YORK NOTES

General Editors: Pr
of Stirling) & Profe
University of Beirui

Edward Albee

WHO'S AFRAID OF VIRGINIA WOOLF?

Notes by Christopher Hudson

MA B PHIL (OXFORD)

LONGMAN
YORK PRESS

YORK PRESS
Immeuble Esseily, Place Riad Solh, Beirut

LONGMAN GROUP UK LIMITED
Longman House, Burnt Mill, Harlow,
Essex CM20 2JE, England
Associated companies, branches and representatives
throughout the world

© Librairie du Liban 1985

First published 1985
Sixth impression 1992

ISBN 0-582-02321-1

Printed in Hong Kong
WLEE/05

Contents

Part 1

Introduction

Albee's childhood and education

Edward Albee was born in 1928. He was abandoned at birth by his natural parents, and it was his fortune, two weeks later, to be adopted by Reed Albee, a millionaire. How good this fortune was may be debated, but it is certain that this circumstance was influential in the career he adopted and left an unmistakable mark upon his writing, which was often to ring the changes upon the themes of the family, adoption and childlessness. Reed Albee's wealth came from a chain of theatres started by his father; and Edward Albee's ambiguous relation to the theatre of his time sprung naturally from his ambiguous relation to his adoptive parents. To them, to the theatre of his time and to society at large he stood in the position of an outsider and critic; destined indeed to make his mark but resistant to any expectation imposed on him. The mixed blessings of his adoption were insufficient to compensate for his abandonment; feelings of resentment and anger formed his maturing mind and personality. Matters were not helped by the particular character of his adoptive family. Reed Albee had married a woman more than twenty years younger and a foot taller than himself. 'I wear the pants in this house because somebody's got to', says Martha in *Who's Afraid of Virginia Woolf?*; to such declarations Edward Albee's childhood memories can have been no stranger: pants, indeed, or more accurately, riding breeches and riding crop feature in his earliest recollections of Mrs Albee. Rejected by his real family and landed in a privileged but eccentric milieu he inevitably lacked a sense of belonging, and it was with a fellow outsider, Mrs Albee's mother, that he felt most kinship. In a pugilistic metaphor, characteristic of his outlook, he says, 'She and I were outside the ring.' Alienation and conflict: these for him were the dominant themes of his early experience, and, later, of his writing.

It comes as no surprise to learn that his experience of formal education was chequered. His first boarding school, Lawrenceville in New Jersey, which he attended from the age of twelve, expelled him after two and a half years. The school had been sympathetic to his peculiar difficulties, and his career there was not without promise, but the energies he devoted to the stage and to school journalism were not matched by achievement in the classroom; he failed four out of five courses and was expelled. A 'military academy'—that last resort of many a desperate American parent—was his next lot. The Valley Forge Military Academy, however, could not detain him long enough to fortify his character in the approved manner, and after little more than a year he moved again. This time he was more fortunate. Choate School, to which he moved next, was an establishment of some distinction, numbering statesmen and public figures among its old boys. Character there was formed by gentler and more urbane methods. Albee became a prolific writer, but not, this time, to the detriment of his formal studies; he stayed at Choate School until he was eighteen, when he left for the university. He attended three universities in all, none of them for long. A reluctance to attend mathematics lectures and chapel ended his brief association with Trinity College, Connecticut. Columbia University and Washington University were no more successful in detaining him; and, only nineteen years old, he was launched upon the world.

Of the institutions that taught him it would seem that Choate School gave him most. He appreciated a regime where discipline consisted of 'letting you come to the conclusion that you were making a fool of yourself', as he described it. But, more important, it was there that he was able to experiment with writing.

Poetry, during this period, was his chief preoccupation and was to remain so for some time to come, but he also wrote short stories, a play, and a novel of substantial length. University life gave him experience of acting and his wide-ranging, if short-lived, experience of the academic milieu bore fruit in *Who's Afraid of Virginia Woolf?*

Apprentice years and American theatre

In the nineteen-fifties for a period of approximately ten years after leaving university and until his reputation as a playwright was established with *The Zoo Story* (1958), Albee's life was desultory and experimental. For a year he continued to live at home, an unsatisfactory arrangement that came to an acrimonious end. At first he wrote for musical programmes on the radio, but he gave that up when he left home. He was also briefly engaged to be married during this year. Setting up home on his own, and comfortably provided for with an unearned income, he embarked upon a series of miscellaneous lowly jobs, being by turns an office boy, record salesman, book salesman, messenger and barman. Throughout this period he continued to write poetry and to experiment with drama.

At the age of thirty, having written *The Zoo Story* which had been successful in production, Albee emerged decisively as a playwright of importance. From then on it was as a playwright that he was known;

the period of experimentation with poetry and other genres was at an end, and, though he continued to experiment within the dramatic form, he had unmistakably found his *métier* and developed a characteristic and confident voice. This is not, however, to dismiss his apprentice years as insignificant. The years at Choate School when he would write for up to eighteen hours a day and fatigue his mentors with voluminous and turgid versifications (which, to their credit, they dutifully appraised), were essential to his subsequent maturing as an individual and as a writer. His output at that time was impressive in its volume alone. Much of this writing has disappeared, though the novel (more than five hundred pages in length) may well be the source of his character George's wistful recollections of an unpublished novel in *Who's Afraid of Virginia Woolf?* Those works which have survived provide some interesting comparisons with his mature work. Professor Bigsby, who has studied his contributions to the Choate literary magazine, has pointed out how his poetry and short stories alike are nourished by adolescent fantasy and illusion to an extent surprising in one whose mature work was to expose and shatter illusion so ruthlessly.* Bigsby has also seen an optimism which continues into his mature work: it is strange to find so all-American an attitude as a permanent theme in such a mordant critic of American society. It seems there is, among his diverse *personae*, an establishment figure, something of a Rotarian even, at work in his rejection of the nihilist who

Existing principles, old trusted ways spikes
And offers in their place sterility
Of soul and thought.

Given the peculiar circumstances of Albee's upbringing it is no wonder that the finding of a distinctive stance and *persona* with a confident voice to match this stance was a lengthy process. The years Albee spent in Greenwich Village in New York after leaving home at nineteen until his first success as a playwright at the age of thirty, were a necessary period of exploration and experiment. It is unlikely that the banal occupations he successively adopted gave him more than a necessary escape from the position of being a poor little rich boy; but these years were not lacking in fruitful intellectual contact. He shared his flat with a composer who was later to write the music for some of his plays, and met through him some literary figures whose advice was valuable. W.H. Auden (1907–73), noticing the prolixity and bombast of his verse, offered timely discouraging advice; while Thornton Wilder (1897–1975), who by an odd chance had once been a master at

* C.W.E. Bigsby, *Albee*, 'Writers and Critics' series, Oliver & Boyd, Edinburgh and London, 1969, pp.2–5.

Lawrenceville, Albee's first boarding school, urged him to turn to drama.

Drama was for him by no means unfamiliar territory. His father's position in the theatrical world probably in some way ensured an awareness in him of the genre and its possibilities from the first. He had written a farce, no longer extant, when he was only twelve. It was mysteriously called *Aliqueen* and was concerned, he recalls, with the conduct of the English gentry on board a liner. When he was eighteen he published a one-act play in the Choate literary magazine. Bigsby observes that the play, while sharing the melodramatic quality of Albee's other early writings and lacking a confident control of dialogue, is nevertheless not without merit and anticipates his later themes. It tells the story of a young man of Irish extraction, who has rejected the Catholic faith of his upbringing, and who persuades a young girl of similar background to adopt his own cynical outlook and later to elope with him. Her crippled grandmother is opposed to the marriage and attempts to prevent their departure by force, falling from her wheelchair in the effort. The young man hustles the grandmother into another room, leaving her to die, reflecting that the pursuit of happiness justifies their conduct. To the assault on a moral cynicism already noticed in his poetry of the period is added an outraged sense that family ties should count for more than they do, a theme to which his mature work returned.

Apart from these early attempts at drama and his family connections with the theatrical milieu, another contribution to his development as a dramatist was his exposure to the intellectual climate of Greenwich Village in the 1950s. This was the period of the Cold War when the confrontation of the West and the communist world had taken on menacing proportions with the development of nuclear armaments. The terrible possibilities of nuclear warfare, which had been demonstrated in Japan at the end of the Second World War, formed an ever-present background to the thinking of the period. Consideration of the insecurity of human life has the effect of raising questions as to its meaning, and this was a period when traditional answers were felt to be inadequate. Academic philosophy had for the most part retreated from metaphysics and comprehensive systems of thought to linguistic philosophy and the study of meaning. Existentialism alone seemed to have something to say about the concerns of that generation. As a philosophic system it was expounded chiefly by the French author Jean-Paul Sartre (1905–80) in works beyond the capacity of the average reader; but the message that filtered through the era was that man's position in the universe was essentially meaningless and that therefore it was for him to create his own meaning. Such an undertaking involves the rejection of all traditional and ready-made systems of religion, morality and social order. Extreme individualism and isolation are inevitable consequences and there was a new interest in the creative literature which dealt with those who stood outside the received ideas of society. During his twenties Albee read the work of writers who share this preoccupation, such as the Irish author Samuel Beckett (*b*. 1906) and the French authors Jean Genet (*b*. 1910) and Eugene Ionesco (*b*. 1912). His own circumstances predisposed him towards them, and they and other writers of neo-existentialist outlook were an essential part of the intellectual climate of Greenwich Village in the 1950s. Albee had a tendency to reject the amorality and nihilism inherent in popular existentialism and he maintained a strong sense of the worth of certain traditional values such as the family. This viewpoint survived his residence in Greenwich Village where the opposite ethos prevailed.

One area where the conflict between received ideas and existentialist experiment was to be found was the theatre itself. The theatrical scene in America may be characterised by a division into Broadway and off-Broadway. Broadway represents the established, essentially commercial theatre, from which Reed Albee had derived his fortune. It was the theatre of which Albee said, in an interview with the British actor Sir John Gielgud,

> The basic crisis the theatre is in now is that the audience primarily wants a reaffirmation of its values, wants to see the status quo, wants to be entertained rather than disturbed, wants to be comforted and doesn't want any kind of adventure in the theatre.*

Off-Broadway, by contrast, was more adventurous, more intellectual. The difference between them may be further characterised by another comment of Albee's in the same interview:

> One season, the following playwrights were not performed in the commercial theatres on Broadway: Becket, Brecht, Genet, Ionesco, O'Casey, de Ghelderode, Shaw, Shakespeare, Strindberg, Ibsen, Chekov. These people were not performed on Broadway; every one of them was performed off Broadway.

Broadway was in decline in the 1950s, both economically and intellectually. The number of theatres in operation had declined steadily for a period of thirty years under competition from the cinema and, later, from television. Of the works performed in the theatres a significant proportion were musicals; of the remainder many were foreign. Thus the centre of American theatre was no longer the centre of a vital indigenous drama.

* R.S. Stewart, 'John Gielgud and Edward Albee talk about the theater', *Atlantic Monthly*, CCXV, iv, pp.61−8. The interview is quoted in full in C.W.E. Bigsby (ed.), *Edward Albee: A Collection of Critical Essays*, Prentice-Hall, Englewood Cliffs, N.J., 1975, pp.14−19.

The giants of American drama, Eugene O'Neill (1888–1953), Arthur Miller (*b.* 1915) and Tennessee Williams (1911–83) were dead or in decline as dramatists. In the experimental off-Broadway theatre vitality was certainly to be found, but from the ferment of ideas and experimentation no unmistakable talent had emerged. At the end of the 1950s Albee stepped into this breach with *The Zoo Story*. After a period of depression, and having given up poetry, he undertook in desperation to write the play 'as a thirtieth birthday present to myself'.

First plays

It is, perhaps, surprising to find that the first performance of *The Zoo Story* was not off Broadway as might have been expected, but at the Berlin Festival of 1959. The play reflects the rebellious beatnik and bohemian works of Greenwich Village with which Albee had been long associated and which was a centre of intellectual revolt. In its self-conscious unorthodoxy, of both message and technique, it would have been typical enough of the experimental theatre in America at that time. It tells the story, if story it can be called, of an encounter on a park bench between a young beatnik called Jerry and a typical middle-class American called Peter. The young beatnik obtrudes his conversation upon the middle-class gentleman, rendering ineffective the latter's defensive barrage of conventional manners and detachment. He insists upon the intimate disclosure of his life in all its somewhat pathetic detail, and is determined to convey the desperation he feels, as he seeks to achieve human contact in an authentic encounter. Trapped by his own rather vapid politeness and good nature the middle-class Peter is drawn reluctantly into his interlocutor's world, and incidentally reveals more of his own world than his conventions would normally allow. In an atmosphere of rising hysteria, Jerry gratuitously provokes Peter to fight with him for possession of the bench.

When Jerry produces a knife and incites Peter to use it, the latter tries to escape. Jerry prevents him and starts to slap him: Peter raises the knife and offers Jerry a last chance to leave him alone. Jerry rushes and impales himself on the knife; as he dies he expresses affection and gratitude to Peter for not rejecting him, and allowing him the contact he sought. As a theatrical piece it is deliberately calculated to affront the expectations of an audience. Apart from its highly dramatic end, and an incident where Jerry tickles Peter, it is devoid of action. Moreover these incidents, by their gratuitously bizarre and irrational nature, frustrate rather than gratify the natural expectations of an audience. Action off-stage there is, as when Jerry describes his visit to the zoo, his love-life, and his encounters with his landlady and her dog. But even here the length and intensity of these narratives are deliberately out of proportion to what would normally be seen as their significance. The play, in short, treats its audience much as Jerry treats Peter; forcing it out of and beyond its conventional responses by a resolute avoidance of normality. In the state of embarrassment and shock it engenders, the audience is open to insights into the significance of what has been witnessed. The skill of the plan consists in the way Jerry succeeds in overcoming Peter's reluctance to be drawn out of his conventional responses; though Jerry is the misfit and the underdog, it is he who takes the initiative throughout. The play, without the usual resources of rationally explicable action, nevertheless commands the attention and responses of the audience. The spectator is left, reluctantly perhaps, admitting the loneliness of the outsider and his desperate quest for meaning and contact in a world without metaphysical certainties.

The figure of the outsider and his rejection of what he would call bourgeois values was a characteristic preoccupation of the 1950s, as is witnessed by the success of Colin Wilson's anthology of popular existentialism entitled *The Outsider* (1956). This preoccupation is implicit in the bohemianism of that period and it gives a dated air to the play. The opposition between Jerry and Peter also reflects the anti-Americanism which is a recurrent theme in Albee's work, and which he admitted to be the subject matter of his play *The American Dream*. The material security which the Peters of this world seek is the characteristic goal of a consumer society. Of the two characters, the bourgeois and bohemian, there can be little doubt which is Mr Average American. The fact that the honours of their bizarre encounter are unmistakably with the bohemian can, with the smallest shift of emphasis, be seen to give the play an anti-American thrust.

The Zoo Story also marks a significant stage in Albee's development of technique. His dependence on monologue to reveal off-stage action is hazardous but generally considered a success. These long narratives of off-stage action were later to be a distinctive feature of *Who's Afraid of Virginia Woolf?* and are, some of them, crucial to the play's power of conviction. Another feature of *The Zoo Story* characteristic of Albee's later work is the opposition that he sees between good manners and truth. Peter is pre-eminently good-mannered and his manners act as a barrier against the realities with which Jerry seeks to confront him. No authentic encounter is possible until this defence has been broken down. The penetrating and insistent impertinence of Jerry's behaviour is more than the mere rudeness of a young man with a chip on his shoulder. It is designed to reveal the reality behind the façade.

In *Who's Afraid of Virginia Woolf?* it is the older man who applies this technique. With devastating skill he penetrates the façade of dignity and detachment of the young lecturer, revealing vulgar ambition and a total lack of principle. Penetration, indeed, is a metaphor the older character, George, uses for the process. He speaks of surgery, cutting through skin, muscles and bone until the knife has penetrated to the marrow (Act III, pp.124−5). In this image of marrow Albee implies that the object of the quest is not`only hard to get, but correspondingly valuable, and the value he sets upon it justifies the process, however disturbing, of its discovery.

In the following year Albee's next play, *The Death of Bessie Smith*, was performed. The idea and the title came from an incident in which the life of a coloured singer, Bessie Smith, might have been saved after an accident but for the fact that the nearest hospital took whites only. This rings the changes on the anti-American theme by exposing racism in some areas of American society. At the time of this play the movement for Civil Rights in the United States still had much to achieve, and the racial problem there was a potentially explosive one during the sixties. In the 1930s, the period in which this play is set, American racism was even more pronounced. Albee sees racism as a facet of the general injustice and inequality to which individuals readily accommodate themselves in their selfish materialistic preoccupations.

In the hospital, where the action of this play mostly takes place, these racial and social injustices are concentrated. There are two converging plots: one concerns the singer Bessie Smith, and the other the relationship between a nurse and an intern at the hospital. We understand from a dialogue between Bessie Smith and her manager Jack that she is about to re-emerge from a period of temporary obscurity. They set off after a drink, for Memphis and then New York. On the road they have an accident. She is taken to the ironically named Mercy Hospital where neither her fame nor her critical condition get her the emergency treatment she needs. There the nurse rejects Jack. The intern, however, does go to examine the singer and returns to report that she is already dead. Jack admits that he knew. That is one of the plots of the play. The other concerns the intern and the nurse. Both of them share a dissatisfaction with the hospital and the unequal way it cares for its patients. This is evidenced in the fuss made over the Mayor who is in for a minor complaint but whose needs are constantly given priority. But the manner in which the nurse's indignation is exposed shows that her democratic spirit does not extend as far as negroes: 'The poor man lying up there with his guts coming out could be a nigger for all the attention he'd get if His Honor should start shouting for something.' We understand, however, that the social conscience of the intern goes further. This doctor is paying court to the nurse with limited encouragement from her: his salary is too low for her to marry him.

For all her dislike of sycophancy towards the Mayor, the nurse encourages the intern to toady to him for the sake of his prospects. He is reluctant to do so. They quarrel so fiercely that she promises to wreck his career, that she has just sought to advance. By going to examine Bessie, thereby contravening the hospital's policy with regard to negroes, he saves her the trouble. The play ends with an hysterical outburst from her in which she rails at him for sacrificing his career for a negro woman.

Like *The Zoo Story* this play shares an unerring instinct for dialogue expressing mixed feelings of hate, love and violence. In the scene between the nurse and her father with which the play opens, and in the later scenes between the nurse and the intern, there is a latent explosiveness of the kind that erupts so arrestingly in *Who's Afraid of Virginia Woolf?* There is an implied criticism, too, of the bourgeois acquisitiveness which characterises Peter, and all he stands for, in *The Zoo Story*. In *The Death of Bessie Smith* this criticism is directed towards the nurse who fails to follow through the dissatisfaction she feels with the values that prevail in the hospital and in society at large. She herself manifests the 'disparity between things as they are and things as they should be' – her own phrase – in her opposition to the intern's idealism and her acceptance of a code which makes a certain financial level a precondition of marriage. One feels that if this couple were to marry, they would mature into something very like George and Martha, with the vivacious product of a consumer society wearing out her husband with chronic discontent, yet pathetically dependent on conflict to sustain their relationship.

With *The Sandbox* and *The American Dream*, performed respectively in 1960 and 1961, Albee developed further the social criticism of *The Zoo Story* and *The Death of Bessie Smith*. The two plays may conveniently be considered together, since, with one exception, the characters of *The Sandbox* appear also in *The American Dream*. *The Sandbox*, which barely lasts a quarter of an hour on the stage, was commissioned while Albee was in the process of writing *The American Dream* for a festival which required a short piece. This accounts for the duplicate use of the characters who, Albee writes, 'were placed in a situation different than (*sic*) but related to their predicament in the longer play'. The characters are undoubtedly drawn from his childhood experience. The dominating wife, the hen-pecked husband and the complaining grandmother, who is nevertheless the most human and sympathetic character portrayed, have their unmistakable parallels in the household of Reed Albee.

In *The Sandbox* the husband and wife, who are designated Mommy and Daddy, bring on Grandma and place her in the sandbox as a kind of burial. She grumbles desultorily, but acquiesces in the arrangement, which is witnessed by a young man who has been doing exercises in the background throughout. He is not only the All-American boy he appears to be, but also the Angel of Death. He announces awkwardly that he 'has come for her'. He kisses Grandma on the forehead and she congratulates him on his performance. That concludes the play. Albee on one level is criticising the reduction of death to bathos and cliché in theatre and cinema; on another, the devaluation of family ties exemplified by the treatment that Grandma has received. It is significant that the All-American Boy is the one who presides over the obsequies, and ironic that she should applaud him for it, though to applaud it as a performance is consistent with her role both inside and outside the play which permits her to comment upon the lighting, refer to the audience and so forth. It suggests that the victims of American society are as much to blame as those who oppress them, a point made in *The Death of Bessie Smith* in the character of the Negro orderly who supports the whites-only status of the hospital.

Social criticism is likewise an element in *The American Dream*. Albee wrote in the preface that

> The play is an examination of the American scene; an attack on the substitution of artificial for real values in our society, a condemnation of complacency cruelty emasculation and vacuity; it is a stand against the fiction that everything in this slipping land of ours is peachy-keen.

The play caused considerable offence, so it may be assumed that Albee's point was taken. As in the case of *The Zoo Story* and *The Sandbox*, the ordinary expectations of an audience, for sequential dialogue and action, are frustrated. Dialogue is deliberately irrational and inconsequent, parodying the emptiness and fatuity of average American middle-class conversation. In the play Mommy and Daddy are awaiting the arrival of a visitor: as they wait, Grandma comes in with a number of boxes, all packed up as though for a final departure. She is expecting someone with a van to take her away. The bell rings and a visitor, Mrs Barker, who is active in voluntary work, arrives. Nonsensical conversation ensues in which it eventually emerges that Mrs Barker, as representative of an adoption society, had arranged the adoption by Mommy and Daddy twenty years earlier of a child, whom they had mutilated. When the child died, they had demanded their money back from the society. Then a handsome and muscular young man, the American Dream in person, enters. Grandma, supposing him to be the van man who has come for her, converses with him and learns that he knew neither of his parents and had suffered the trauma of separation from an identical twin. Grandma arranges with Mommy and Daddy to adopt this young man, who is not the van man but the twin of the boy they had adopted twenty years previously. This proposal is joyfully accepted by all, whereupon Grandma brings down the curtain with the comment that everyone has what they want or think they want.

In these two plays Albee's experimentation takes him close to a loosely defined type of drama known as the Theatre of the Absurd. Already in *The Zoo Story* he had moved in that direction: in these two plays and certain later works he moved closer still. Some characteristics of this work are similar to those of *The Zoo Story*. They consist chiefly of an inconsequence of dialogue and action conveying a sense that no real communication is achieved when people speak to each other, and that what they do neither arises from their circumstances nor impinges upon them. Writers whose thinking influenced Albee during the fifties, Samuel Beckett, Jean Genet and Eugene Ionesco, use this theatrical style to express a nihilist or existentialist world-view. As the critic Martin Esslin writes in *The Theatre of the Absurd* (1961):

> Behind the satirical exposure of inauthentic ways of life the theatre of the absurd is facing up to a different level of absurdity in the absurdity of the human condition itself in a world where the decline of religious belief has deprived man of certainties.

Albee does not seem to adhere to this kind of nihilism. In the plays discussed above, social criticism implies the validity of certain values which are seen to be lacking: humanity, justice, family ties and an opposition to crass materialism. Furthermore, his plays have distinguishable endings. Events, we feel, have arrived, when the curtain falls, at a significant point. Jerry's death in *The Zoo Story* is conclusive in every sense of the word and its meaning is made explicit in his final speech. In *The Sandbox* the Angel of Death comes for Grandma: in *The American Dream* glasses are raised to celebrate the adoption, and Grandma announces to the audience that 'That just about wraps it up.'

Absurdism in its purest form allows no such conclusiveness: where events have no meaning and are not determined by the ordinary laws of cause and effect, there cannot be beginnings, middles and ends. Albee, then, exploits some of the mannerisms of absurdism without accepting its philosophic basis. Inanities and inconsequence of dialogue and gesture, such as he employs in *The American Dream*, have a powerful satiric effect but the point they make is that a particular society has lost touch with the meaning of life rather than that life has no meaning.

Who's Afraid of Virginia Woolf?

Who's Afraid of Virginia Woolf?, first performed in 1961, was Albee's next work. It was highly successful and created a gratifying degree of outrage. That it was first performed on Broadway, the centre of conventional drama, must have been no less gratifying to Albee, the butts of whose mordant wit were more likely to be found there than in the avant-garde theatres off Broadway. The play was nominated for the Pulitzer prize, but two members of the committee resigned in protest and this prevented it from being considered. It was for a later work, *A Delicate Balance*, that Albee finally received the honour in 1967. *Who's Afraid of Virginia Woolf?* was performed in London, and successfully filmed, and its progress from *succès de scandale* to examination text has taken less than two decades. A detailed appraisal of its qualities is contained in Part 3 of these Notes. Here we will describe what it shares with the work that preceded it. In *The Zoo Story* and *The Death of Bessie Smith* there are pairs of characters who change each other, and their relationships, by a process of friction. In *The Zoo Story* this happens between strangers; in *The Death of Bessie Smith*, between lovers. In both cases a crisis is precipitated. This process of inducing a crisis is central in *Who's Afraid of Virginia Woolf?*, and by the time he wrote it Albee had a confident mastery of the kind of repartee upon which it depends. The fierce virtuosity of its dialogue is the play's most striking quality and the one most likely to perpetuate its reputation. Social criticism, which is a central element in all the earlier plays, is also present in *Who's Afraid of Virginia Woolf?*, but as a more peripheral theme. Albee's affinities with the theatre of the absurd which are so apparent in *The Zoo Story, The Sandbox* and *The American Dream* can be traced in certain dramatic mannerisms and in some of the preoccupations of the play, but it is in a manifestly different category.

Later development

Albee's subsequent work does not concern us here, though a list of his works appears in Part 5. His position as a leading American playwright was assured after the success of *Who's Afraid of Virginia Woolf?*, though, characteristically, he resisted the expectations of those who envisaged an immediate succession of triumphs in the same mould. It was a source of disappointment to some that he was content to adapt the work of others for production, as he did in *The Ballad of Sad Café*, which followed the success of *Who's Afraid of Virginia Woolf?* The Broadway success of *Who's Afraid of Virginia Woolf?* did not end his commitment to the experimental theatre, as *The Box* and *Quotations from Mao Tse Tung* show. But more orthodox successes such as *A Delicate Balance* have not been wanting and Albee has continued to build upon the reputation won for him by *Who's Afraid of Virginia Woolf?* as one of the most arresting and vital voices in current American literature.

A note on the text

Who's Afraid of Virginia Woolf? was first published in New York in 1962, both by the Dramatist's Play Service and by Atheneum. In 1963 a further edition was published in New York in the Pocket Book series. Versions are available also in a number of anthologies put out by American publishers. The play was first published in Britain by Jonathan Cape, London, in 1964. A paperback edition was published by Penguin Books, Harmondsworth, in 1965 and has been reprinted sixteen times since then. This Penguin edition is readily available and the page references in these Notes are to it.

Part 2

Summaries

of WHO'S AFRAID OF VIRGINIA WOOLF?

A general summary

Who's Afraid of Virginia Woolf? is set in a small American university on the East Coast. It is concerned with the events of one night, during which two couples stay up drinking after a party given by the President of the University for the teaching staff. For both couples the quarrels and revelations of the night bring to a head a number of issues which had been unresolved in their respective relationships. The upheavals both marriages undergo are so violent and destructive that neither can be the same again. Although it is clear that the future for both couples will be difficult, Albee implies that they are free to build upon a foundation more solid than the pretences and deceptions which have supported their marriages so far.

The characters whose marriage is the main subject of the play are George and Martha. George is in his late forties, a history professor at the university. He is disillusioned and unsuccessful in his career. His wife is the daughter of the President of the university, and it had originally been the President's plan to groom George as his successor. George, however, has long since shown himself to be inadequate for this role, and even failed to become head of the history department. His wife, Martha, who is some years older, is disappointed by his failure and nags him continually. They have no children. In common, it seems, with the rest of the university they both drink heavily, and she, at least, seeks sexual adventure outside the marriage.

This unpromising relationship is held together in two ways. One is that George and Martha seek stimulus in quarrelling and psychological cruelty. They do this quite deliberately by tacit agreement, as a kind of game. The other is that they indulge a pretence that they have a son, concerning whom they converse, making imaginary plans and enjoying imaginary reminiscences. This, unlike their quarrels which are sometimes public, is private.

The other couple are Nick and Honey. Although their relationship is not the main focus of the play, it duplicates some of the features in that of George and Martha. Like George and Martha, they have no children. For them, too, the events of the night expose old deceptions and illusions, thereby freeing them to make a new start. Nick and Honey are new to the university, and are meeting George and Martha for the first time. The two couples are in strong contrast. Nick is young, vigorous and full of ambition: he has a record of precocious academic success behind him and is a former athlete of distinction. His wife is infertile and drinks heavily, and is only partially aware of what happens around her.

When the play begins George and Martha are set for a quarrelsome evening as they wait for their guests to arrive. The only hint of restraint comes in an unexpectedly serious warning by George not to reveal their fantasy about having a son. Martha, in a defiant mood, appears to reject the warning. Nick and Honey arrive in the middle of the quarrel, which George and Martha do not attempt to conceal. Although the former are embarrassed and make half-hearted attempts to leave, they are persuaded to stay, and are drawn into the quarrel. It is clear that the restraints of ordinary politeness will have no place in this encounter. From the start, then, no holds are barred, and the scene is set for the upheavals which are the main concern of the play.

The play is divided into three acts, entitled, respectively, 'Fun and Games', 'Walpurgisnacht' and 'Exorcism', these titles being an indication of the course of the action of the play.

The 'Fun and Games' of the first act consist in the characters probing and exposing each others' weak points. In this act Martha reveals George's failure, which George himself sardonically endorses in discussion with Nick. Martha flirts with Nick, openly contrasting him with her husband. George refuses to be provoked, pretending indifference. He reacts to Nick with controlled hostility, expressing a distaste for Nick's subject, biology, and accusing him of wanting to establish a totalitarian society by means of eugenics. Meanwhile he has noted that Nick has no children and that his 'slim-hipped' wife is not a maternal type. He suspects, as it proves rightly, that there is more to this than meets the eye. And, most important of all, it emerges during this act that Martha has spoken to Honey about their 'son', thus forcing them both to sustain the pretence publicly.

The second act, 'Walpurgisnacht', is so named after the German tradition of the night of St Walpurga, in May, when ghosts are believed to walk. The 'ghosts' that have been raised by the 'Fun and Games' of the first act now walk the stage at large in all their destructive force. George, for example, follows up his suspicion that all is not well between Nick and Honey. While they are alone together he encourages Nick to recount the circumstances of his marriage, namely that Nick had married Honey believing her to be pregnant, only to discover that the 'pregnancy' was no more than a hysterical symptom. He then recounts this story in front of Nick and Honey on her return, pretending that it is the plot of an unpublished novel of his, and causing the utmost embarrassment. The flirtation between Nick and Martha develops. George continues to pretend indifference until Nick and Martha leave the stage to make love. In their absence George resolves to 'kill' the imaginary son by announcing to them all that he has died in a car accident.

Just as George has been forced to keep up the pretence of the son's existence once Martha has mentioned him, so Martha will be forced to accept the pretence of his death once George has announced it before the others. The fantasy which has sustained their marriage will thus be finally destroyed.

The final act is called 'Exorcism' because the ghosts that walked in Act II are laid to rest in Act III. We learn that Nick, being drunk, has failed to make love to Martha. George draws Martha on to talk of the son and at a certain point begins to speak the Latin words of the Roman Catholic burial service. After an elaborate preamble he announces the death of the 'son', claiming to have received a telegram to that effect while Nick and Martha were off stage. He ignores Martha's plea that this breaks the 'rules of the game' and continues to act as if the son, and his death, are real. The mention of a son prompts Honey to announce that she wants a child: a change from her selfish and neurotic avoidance of childbearing to date. As Nick and Honey leave Martha and George soberly discuss how they will, from now on, face a life unsupported by illusion.

Detailed summaries

In this play the acts are not divided up into scenes. For the purposes of these summaries, therefore, the divisions of each act are indicated by page references and correspond to the natural divisions and shifts of the action and dialogue. Page references follow the Penguin edition of the text.

Act I   pages 11—19

This section, beginning when Martha and George return from the party and ending with the arrival of the guests, serves to introduce George and Martha and to indicate the kind of relationship they have. It establishes that Martha is older than George, a heavy drinker, aggressive in manner and still sexually vivacious. It establishes George as passive, indifferent and cynical about his wife's outrageous behaviour. It indicates also that a quarrelsome tone is habitual between them and that they criticise each other's faults without restraint. Finally, it emphasises the importance to them both of the 'bit about the kid,' though its exact nature is as yet unexplained, and we learn that, whatever it is, Martha will not agree to keep it secret.

NOTES AND GLOSSARY:

Martha and George: the names are established early in the play. They are the names of the founder President of the United States, George Washington and his wife. Albee has told us that this was deliberate, and that a critique of American society is one of the themes of the play, though not the central one

cluck: fool

Bette Davis: (*b*. 1908) an American film actress of the period

dump: squalid, untidy or otherwise disagreeable place

dumbbell: a fool or dullard

peritonitis: a potentially fatal condition, usually following appendicitis

that was probably before my *time*: George teases Martha for being older than he is

bray: this comparison of Martha's voice to a donkey's indicates George's distaste for her over-aggressive, extroverted manner

and good-looking: George has guessed that Martha has invited the man because she is attracted to him. The implication is that this behaviour is characteristic

a mousey little type, without any hips, or anything: this emphasis upon the girl's unmaternal and unfeminine appearance becomes significant later, when we learn the real circumstances of her childlessness

Daddy said we should be nice to them: it is significant that Martha says and repeats this as though it concluded the argument. The implication is that her father dominates their life and that George has no will of his own

Georgie-Porgie, put-upon pie: Martha adapts a line from a nursery rhyme 'Georgie-porgie pudding and pie'. 'Put upon' means forced to do things against his will, in this case to entertain her guests

Who's afraid of Virginia Woolf: this song, which recurs as a theme throughout the play, is an adaptation of the nursery rhyme 'Who's afraid of the big bad wolf?' There is no particular significance in the substitution of the novelist's name for the last four words. This, at any rate, appears to have been the view of the producer of a performance which took place in Prague under the title of *Who's Afraid of Franz Kafka?* Albee, who originally found the title ready-made, inscribed on a wall in a public place, has informed us that for him they mean 'Who is afraid of a life without illusions?' We need not assume that they bear that meaning on every occasion of their occurrence

puke: vomit

simp: simpleton or idiot

you're going bald . . . (*pause . . . then they both laugh*): this shows that George and Martha engage in this kind of quarrelling not, as would seem natural, as an expression of mutual hatred, but because they find it stimulating and enjoyable. At the end of this bout they seem pleased with each other

There isn't an abomination award going . . . : in a competition for any kind of bad behaviour you would always win

your *heads*, I should say: the implication is that Martha is a monster

don't start on the bit . . . : that is, don't introduce the subject of . . . . He doesn't say what subject but he means the subject of their imaginary child

---

Act I   pages 19–25

This section extends from the arrival of Nick and Honey, the guests, to the exits of Martha and Honey. Although Martha and George are in effect meeting their guests for the first time they make no attempt to avoid embarrassing them with their quarrel. This sets the tone for an evening uninhibited by ordinary politeness. It is particularly hard for Nick and Honey to know how to react to George's open dislike of the President of the university, his father-in-law. Again George tells Martha, as she shows Honey to the bathroom, to keep silent about a subject which he doesn't specify, but which is the matter of their imaginary son. Again she refuses.

NOTES AND GLOSSARY:

Nick and Honey: from the choice of names given to the main characters (George and Martha) and Albee's admission of their significance (see note, p.21 above), we may deduce that no names given to his characters are wholly without significance. Albee himself has suggested that Nick is so called after Nikita Khrushchev, the Soviet leader of that time. Soviet Russia, is of course, an example of a totalitarian state based upon a utopian ideal and there is emphasis throughout the play on Nick's ambitions as a biologist to create a utopian society. Honey is

not usually a name, merely an expression of
endearment: as such it is suitable for so insub-
stantial a personality as Honey

sour-puss: ill-tempered person. Martha is drawing attention
to George's annoyance at the arrival of the guests.
It is not surprising that Nick thinks they should
leave. Without, however, ceasing to quarrel with
George, Martha insists on their staying

joshed: teased or made fun of. George is putting nonsensical art critics' jargon into Nick's mouth
before hearing precisely what he has to say about
the picture

Bourbon on the rocks: American whiskey with ice

rubbing alcohol: alcohol for medical purposes is stronger than any
drink. A reference to Martha's drunkenness

brandy Alexanders...: these are the names of exotic cocktails.
Martha still likes strong drink but is now
indifferent to the taste

craw: stomach. In the context, the phrase has no meaning and is probably intended by George for
rhetorical effect, albeit unsuccessful

down the hatch: an invitation to drink. Not usual in civilised society

Dylan Thomas-y quality that gets me right where I live: Martha is
mocking George's rhetoric, ironically comparing it
to the poetry of Dylan Thomas (1914–53) and
ironically maintaining that she finds it sexually
exciting

bust a gut: laugh so vigorously as to cause internal injury

And you'd better believe it!: George implies that Martha's father must
be idolised by anyone who hopes to succeed in the
university

a somewhat more private portion of the anatomy: the testicles. George
means that his masculinity is undermined by his
position as son-in-law of the president, presumably
because it seems that his status is due to Martha
and not to his own abilities

the euphemism: here, for lavatory. George mocks Honey for her
excessively genteel refusal to say plainly what she
wants

don't shoot your mouth off: don't be indiscreet. We have not yet
learnt what it is George wants her to keep secret,
except that it is 'about the kid' (see note on 'don't
start on the bit', p.22 above)

Act I   pages 25–32

This section extends from the point where the ladies exit until they return. George and Nick are alone in conversation. George is deliberately offensive. His motives are not explained: we may guess that it is part of his quarrelling with his wife to insult guests whom she has invited. Also it is a theme of the play, and indeed of much of Albee's work, that normal politeness precludes real contact between people. To get beyond Nick's social responses is necessary in order to discover the truth about him, and for this aggression is a necessary preliminary. But in the light of later events it is evident that he is jealous.

George recognises a threat in Nick, whose youth, energy and optimism contrast with his own premature senility, apathy and disillusion, to which he often refers. There is symbolic force, too, in the different subjects they teach. George's subject is history, Nick's biology. The one is concerned exclusively with the past, the other has implications for the future, which are constantly emphasised here. George, as a historian, can only record and reflect on human life, whereas Nick as a biologist can control it. George's fear and resentment of this aspect of Nick's work is another contributory factor in his jealousy. And, of course, George knows, we may assume, from long experience, that his wife finds Nick sexually attractive precisely because of these differences and will humiliate him if she can. Such suspicions are confirmed when she reappears, seductively dressed in different clothes.

As if in anticipation of such an event, George uses every possible means to put Nick at a disadvantage. He embarrasses him but prevents his leaving; he deliberately misunderstands him, not allowing him to explain himself, throwing his own words back at him, interrupting him and disconcertingly changing the subject. He discovers, furthermore, that Nick and Honey have no children, but refuses to say whether he and Martha have any. The stage directions in this section indicate the manner and purpose of George's remarks and Nick's reaction to them.

NOTES AND GLOSSARY:

Parnassus: in Greek mythology, the mountain of the Muses, goddesses of learning and the arts in their various branches. In so describing the house of the University president, George is ironically calling the place a centre of culture, which it should be, but isn't

l'il ol' Martha: an expression of endearment and affection, again meant ironically

bested: defeated. This view of himself and his career is characteristic of George's disillusioned outlook

I'm sorry if we . . . : the sentence would normally be expected to end '. . . have come at an inconvenient time', or in

some similar expression, which could act as an
excuse for taking leave. Other instances of the
same kind are found on page 27: 'When my wife
comes down I think we'll just . . . ' and 'I do think
that when my wife comes downstairs . . . '. These
are likewise interrupted by George, who thus
manages to keep the guests from leaving. Compare
also the stage direction '*undecided*' when Nick says
'Still . . . ' George skilfully changes the subject and
the pace (see stage directions)

musical beds: there is a game called musical chairs where players
race to occupy a limited number of chairs when
the music stops. George means that in the university couples exchange beds as readily; that is, they
are promiscuous

abmaphid: the progression from Bachelor's to Master's to
Doctor's degrees; that is, the course of a university
education. George's remark means that he is
uncertain whether a university education is good (a
'wonder drug') or bad (a 'wasting disease of the
frontal lobes' – a part of the brain). This is characteristic of his disillusionment with his career

thirty-six, twenty-two, seventy-eight men: men who are attracted to
women with excessively large hips. The figures here
represent measurement in inches, before the metric
system was universally adopted in the English-
speaking world. The measurements are of bust,
waist and hips in that order. The measurements
here given are those of a well-proportioned woman
with the exception of the last, the hip measurement, which is approximately twice as large as it
should be. George means that although he does not
like large hips in women, Honey's are too small
even for his taste. He also means that her physique
is unsuited to child bearing

Illyria . . . Penguin Island . . . Gomorrah: Illyria is the scene of Shake-
speare's *Twelfth Night*, and is therefore used as an
imaginary ideal place, as is Penguin Island.
Gomorrah was a city on the Dead Sea, referred to
in the Bible as a place of great immorality which
was destroyed by divine judgement (see Genesis,
chs 18 and 19). George implies that an immoral
place might be Nick's ideal

New Carthage: though the name is fictional the choice of Carthage is significant, because in antiquity that city had a reputation for immorality, deriving from St Augustine (354−430), who wrote of it in his *Confessions* (Book III), 'To Carthage I came, where there sang all around me in my ears a cauldron of unholy loves.'

Micronesian tortoises: tortoises from certain groups of islands in the South Pacific, collectively known as Micronesia, live to a great age

---

Act I   pages 32−57

This section extends from the return of Martha and Honey till the end of the act. In it the four characters are all together on stage. The hostilities indicated in the two preceding sections, the old one between George and Martha and the new one between George and Nick, are developed.

Martha's first act of war is to return dressed with deliberate seductiveness, thereby revealing her intentions towards Nick. The next is that she has revealed the existence of the 'son' to Honey, who speaks of him in front of them all, thereby forcing George to sustain the pretence along with her. She tells the story of a boxing accident in which she knocked George down, which shows him in a ridiculous light. George retaliates dramatically with a realistic pretence of attempted murder in which he shoots a gun which merely emits a parasol. While the other characters are temporarily shocked, Martha is delighted in a way that illustrates the curious, sado-masochistic nature of their relationship, in which both partners relish violence and enjoy subjecting each other to pain, fear or humiliation. She starts to make up to George, but when he rejects her she resumes her flirtation with Nick in earnest, by way of revenge. Deliberately she flatters him for the very thing which George dislikes, namely his subject, biology. The subject has physical (and by extension) sexual content which appeals to her: it is, in her phrase, 'at the meat of things'. She flatteringly compares Nick to the ideal supermen whom George accuses him of intending to create. George retaliates by forcing Martha to answer Honey's questions about the 'son': Martha claims that George is uncertain that he is the father. Further opportunity for humiliating George occurs when the subject changes to Martha's father: she recounts the story of her courtship of George and his inadequacy for the role she and her father had planned for him. Her narrative is halted when George smashes a bottle and drowns her voice by singing 'Who's Afraid of Virginia Woolf'. Honey departs to vomit, and the act ends.

NOTES AND GLOSSARY:

You to know and me to find out: Nick is throwing back George's own words at him when the latter declined to tell Nick whether he had children or not

O.K., Martha: George, on learning that Martha has revealed the secret of their 'son', is thinking of revenge

Sunday chapel dress: an ironical comment. A dress for chapel would be modest and sober. The dress into which Martha has changed is not

barie poo: bar, in baby language

rapport... established: (*stage directions*): they acknowledge that there is a relationship between them

George, here, doesn't cotton much to body talk: George doesn't enjoy discussion of physiques (because he himself is senile and unfit). Martha is deliberately annoying him by admiring Nick's physique and athleticism

bloody-up his meal ticket: injure the man who was responsible for ·paying him

roundhouse right: a swing with the right fist

You liked that, did you?: this incident and Martha's reaction to it indicate her taste for violence and the part it plays in enlivening their relationship

blue games: indecent games

Fat chance: improbable. Martha means that George lacks the energy and enterprise to murder her

You don't need any props: she means that Nick is sexually exciting in himself and requires no extra apparatus like George

chromosomes: part of a cell responsible for determining the characteristics, including the sex, of an embryo. Because of their connection (to the non-specialist at least) with sexuality Martha expresses enthusiasm for them

scrotum: part of the male genitals

I known when I'm being threatened: the threat to George is on two levels. On the personal level Nick is set to succeed in the university where George has failed, and is attractive to Martha as George apparently is not. On the wider level Nick represents, in his own words, 'the wave of the future'. As a biologist he will have a part in the creation of a scientifically controlled utopia, such as Aldous Huxley's (1894–1963) *Brave New World* (1932) envisaged. George, as a historian, is backward-looking and

	sees all that he values in civilisation under threat from such a utopia
I'm sorry I brought it up:	George turns the argument by punning on the two senses of the expression 'to bring up'. Martha means that she regrets mentioning the subject. George takes it in the sense of raise or educate; that is why he insists that 'him' and not 'it' is the appropriate object of the verb
floozie:	a disreputable woman
S.O.B.:	son of a bitch
endowment:	the amount of money owned by the university
Lady Chatterley arrangement:	in D.H. Lawrence's (1885–1930) novel, *Lady Chatterley's Lover* (1928), the heroine has an affair with a social inferior
annulled:	in marriage law annulment means that the 'marriage' is reckoned not to have been a marriage at all and is therefore legally cancelled
barely with it:	(*stage direction*) hardly understanding what is going on
hooch:	alcohol
dumb cluck:	silly fool
the other business:	he means the secret of their 'son'
sprung a leak:	revealed a secret; that is, about the 'son'
flop:	failure

Act II   pages 58–74

Except for a brief reappearance by Martha, in this section Nick and George are alone together again while Martha attends to Honey who has just been sick. They continue to drink heavily: as a result their conversation becomes increasingly inconsequent but their hostility continues and George, at least, is more alert than might appear. He tells Nick a story, purporting to be of his schooldays, in which he and some schoolfriends get drunk for the first time: a character features in it who had killed both father and mother in separate accidents. (Later in the act this incident is referred to as the plot of an unpublished novel by George.) This reminiscence extracts, in turn, a confidence from Nick: he admits how he came to be married and how he proposes to advance his career in the university. In the hands of an enemy these admissions are potentially damaging. Nick's relationship with his wife, we learn, is built upon inadequate and discreditable foundations. They had been childhood friends and had engaged in immature exploration together ('playing doctors', as Nick, in a man-to-man vein, confides). Moreover, before their marriage Honey had had what is described as an hysterical pregnancy: without being actually pregnant, she had exhibited all the symptoms of being so. In these circumstances, Nick was obliged to marry her. After the marriage the 'pregnancy' had proved to be a false alarm. Nick appears to have been reconciled to this by the consideration that Honey had inherited a considerable fortune from her father, a travelling evangelist of evidently dubious character.

These circumstances and Honey's habits and character preclude any real passion in the marriage, and it is not surprising that in such a marriage Nick should be prepared to be unfaithful, especially in the interests of his career. George leads him on to admit, albeit jocularly, that he proposes to sleep with those women whose influence might further his ambition. George makes use of these admissions later, to Nick's great embarrassment.

NOTES AND GLOSSARY:

rest home: an establishment for the treatment of alcoholics

can it: stop it, shut up

hacking away . . . red in the face and winded, missing half the time: George is comparing himself and Martha to two unfit boxers performing incompetently. The comparison of their relationship to a boxing match is apt and recurs several times

throws up: vomits

hysterical pregnancy: a medical condition, uncommon but not unknown, in which a woman, mistakenly supposing herself to be pregnant, develops the symptoms of pregnancy such as a distended stomach, without being pregnant in fact

Punic Wars: events in 2nd and 3rd-century BC Roman history, and thus a sardonic reference by George to his age. The Punic Wars were fought against Carthage and the town where the play is set is called New Carthage. No special significance beyond accidental association of ideas need be attached to this

Great Experiment, or Prohibition: a period in the United States from 1919 to 1933 during which the sale of alcohol was forbidden

bergin: he meant gin; the joke appears to have been that in the Prohibition he had grown up in ignorance of its name and also of the fact that it is not normally taken with water. It may also be that the similarity in sound between 'bergin' and 'virgin' contributed to the joke: alternatively the word is a conflation of bourbon (whiskey) and gin

testy: short-tempered

Cyclops: in Greek mythology the Cyclops was a monster with one eye. George refers to Martha as a monster on more than one occasion

Monstre, Cochon, Bête, Canaille, Putain: French for, respectively, monster, pig, beast, rascal, whore

archery: shooting with bow and arrow. George means that his guesswork was accurate

flip: flippant or cynical

Chinese women: in some sectors of American society it is mistakenly supposed that the vulva of the Chinese woman is horizontal and not vertical

freshen you up: refill your glass

wave-of-the-future boys: George has an idea that Nick, as a biologist, wishes to establish a totalitarian utopia on eugenic principles, as envisaged in Huxley's *Brave New World*. He therefore interprets all Nick's actions as being motivated by the desire to obtain power, and expresses an interest in the tactics ('methodology ...pragmatic accommodation') by which this is to be achieved. Marrying for money, for George, is an example of this

starting in: becoming aggressive

just this much for Martha: George indicates with finger and thumb that the amount was so small as to be almost nothing

priest ... man of God: Nick probably means that Honey's father was Protestant, not Catholic, and is expressing a characteristic mid-western prejudice against Catholics

get the goods on you: find out your discreditable secrets to use against you

find the weak spots, shore 'em up, but with my own name plate on 'em: Nick means that he will put right what is wrong in his department (for example, take over the teaching of courses that are at present unsatisfactory) and thus get control of increasing areas of the department's work

plough a few pertinent wives: sleep with the wives of men who are important and influential in the university. This admission is made as a joke, but it explains how he comes to be seduced by Martha. As daughter of the President she is the most 'pertinent' of all

the way to a man's heart is through his wife's belly: a variation on the proverb that the way to a man's heart is through his stomach, that is, a woman can win a man's love by feeding him well. What George is saying is that to influence a man you must sleep with his wife. Again, though they are joking, what they say appears to be true of this society and of Nick's motives

ladies of the night: prostitutes

mount her like a goddamn dog: again these words are meant as a joke, but George throws them back at Nick later in the play when they prove true of him

Everything's going to work out anyway, because the timetable's history: George is taunting Nick for his supposed confidence that the future belongs to people like himself and that everything will inevitably turn out according to his programme

up yours: an indecent expression of dismissal and contempt. Nick is rejecting George's attempt to warn him not to pursue his ambitions with the disregard for principles and civilised values that he has betrayed

Dies Irae: (*Latin*): literally the Day of Wrath or Judgement, at the end of the world, which is announced by the sound of a trumpet. The words are also the title of a section of the Roman Catholic Requiem Mass (see note on 'Absolve, Domine . . . ', p.39 below). In musical settings this section frequently features a trumpet

Act II   pages 74–84

When the four characters are together again an argument arises between George and Martha, each blaming the other for the 'son's' supposed sicknesses and delinquencies. George accuses Martha of continual sexual assaults on him. Martha raises the topic of George's novel, unpublished because of her father's objection to it, but Honey intervenes with the suggestion that they should dance. Martha welcomes this idea because it will further her flirtation with Nick, but George sabotages it temporarily by putting on a Beethoven symphony, which, however, does not deter Honey from dancing absurdly on her own. When stopped, she sulks, so it is left to Martha and Nick to dance together, which they do, with increasing intimacy. During the course of their dance Martha enlarges, in impromptu verse, on the subject of George's unpublished novel. The subject of this novel is the story which George told Nick (see Act II, p.61) about a boy who had killed both his father and mother in separate accidents. George, enraged, stops the record, but fails to stop Martha telling Nick that it was supposed to be autobiographical.

In George's earlier account of this incident the character concerned could not have been George himself because after the second accident the boy had become chronically dumb. In Martha's account, the implication in George's claim that the novel was autobiographical is that George himself had killed both parents. Certainly Nick so understands it. George attacks Martha; after a scuffle, Nick restores order.

NOTES AND GLOSSARY:

bergin: see note, p.29 above. Martha's reference to the story indicates that she finds opportunity for annoying George in connection with it. We are soon to learn that she blames George for giving in to her father who had forbidden him to publish the novel of which this is the plot

Mixed doubles: George means, how are they to pair up for dancing? He suggests that each should partner the other's husband or wife

Sacre du Printemps: a ballet by the Russian composer Igor Stravinski (1882–1971), notable for its erotic intensity. As such, George implies it would appeal to Martha

it's a familiar dance . . . it's a very old ritual: George means that their dance is suggestive of the sexual act

not entirely with it: (*stage direction*) not knowing what is going on

something funny in his past: presumably the accident in which his father and mother were killed, as described in George's long reminiscence to Nick (see Act II, p.61). In that account it is not George's father and mother who were killed, whereas in Martha's account it appears to be. Nick certainly understands it that way, because he later challenges George with it to test the truth of another story involving George's parents (Act III, p.118). It is clear that one or other or both of George's stories are false, but this is never cleared up. The uncertainty is deliberate, contributing to the theme that it is not easy to distinguish between truth and illusion

Act II   pages 84–91

George, seriously unnerved, tries to re-establish himself by suggesting further 'games'. 'Humiliate the Host' is over: he now proposes 'Hump the Hostess', referring to Nick and Martha's flirtation. When everyone is embarrassed, he proposes instead 'Get the Guests'. He surprises Martha by talking of another unpublished novel and immediately launches into a satirical account of Nick's marriage. He tells how they were childhood friends and that they had played 'doctors'; he tells how her father came by his money; and he tells how Nick married her, mistakenly supposing her to be pregnant. Honey's vagueness and naïveté make her slower than Nick to realise whom the story is about. She encourages George to continue. Nick is unable to stop him and Honey eventually recognises herself in the story, and naturally is disgusted at Nick for revealing the matter to strangers. Honey leaves the room to be sick again and Nick goes to attend to her.

NOTES AND GLOSSARY:

hump: to copulate with. Earlier (see note on 'mount her like a goddamn dog', p.31 above) Nick has half-jocularly expressed such an intention

book dropper: George is referring to Martha's recital of the story of his unpublished novel. It is parallel to her revelation of the secret about their 'son'

You can't fly on one game: one game is not enough

bucolic: a story of country people. To sophisticated New Englanders, such as George and Martha, people from further west such as Nick and Honey appear rustic

a travelling clip joint, based on Christ and all those girls: George is giving as unfavourable account as possible of Nick and Honey, the game being 'Get the Guests'. Here he is exploiting the similarity between some forms of American religious revivalism and travelling shows. He implies that Honey's father's enterprise was immoral and highly profitable

frau: (*German*) wife

Historical inevitability: in their earlier arguments George had accused Nick of supposing that history was on his side and that as a biologist he would have a leading role in the new civilisation biologists are to create

champeen: champion. George is contemptuously mimicking a western accent

simp: simpleton

a swine to show you where the truffles are: truffles are found with the aid of pigs who can locate them with their sense of smell. The 'truffles' here are Nick's and Honey's secret and George is implying that Nick is a pig to reveal them

I'll play the charades like you set them up: 'I will act the role you are casting me for', that is, he will pursue his ambition without principle, including the seduction of Martha for the sake of his career

Act II   pages 91–96

Martha and George are left alone together. Martha applauds George for showing some life at last but derides him for attacking such second-rate people. They quarrel about their whole marriage and their use of quarrelling to enliven it. Amid recriminations they agree that this is a turning point: from now on, in George's words, it is to be 'total war'.

NOTES AND GLOSSARY:

if quarterback there is a pigmy...: George is referring to Nick. Quarterback is a position in American football: he is therefore referring to Nick's athletic physique which is by no means that of a pigmy

you'll wish you'd died in that automobile: the one in which George supposedly killed his father. We need not infer from this that the story is more than fantasy

your·dirty underthings in public: the public revelation of private matters

frigging...convoluted: excessively complicated. 'Frigging' is slang for masturbating. It is here used merely as an indecent expletive

committed: shut up on the grounds of insanity or alcoholism

maybe tomorrow he'll be dead: Martha presumably refers to her father, whom, she believes, George makes an excuse for his failure

Act II   pages 96–108

When Nick returns from looking after Honey, the 'total war' agreed upon begins to take shape. For Martha it takes the form of resuming her seduction of Nick while George is momentarily out of the room. For George it takes the form of pretending not to care at all. This makes Martha first suspicious, and then, when he calmly settles down to read, furious. She sends Nick to wait for her in the kitchen and tries to shake George out of his pose of indifference. He continues indifferent, so she goes to the kitchen to make love with Nick. When she is out he gives way to the fury he really feels, and flings the book away. It hits the doorbell the sound of which brings Honey back. She is drunk and half sleep-talking, and reveals that she is scared to have children. George realises that she has been secretly aborting and accuses her of it.

She refuses to understand what her husband is doing, and continues to ask about the bells. This gives George an idea: he decides to tell Martha that the bells rang when someone called with a telegram announcing their 'son's' death. He tells Honey, and practises announcing it to Martha as his next act of war.

NOTES AND GLOSSARY:

mugging: making a face

ice for the lamps of China: in Imperial China ice was used to reflect the light of torches. George is so unnerved by Martha's behaviour that his conversation is incoherent at this point

the worm turns: the proverb is that a worm if trodden on will turn, that is, no one can be persecuted indefinitely without taking action. She says it does not apply to George: he will never turn ('You are in a straight line'), though she admits that the comparison with a worm is apt enough

up to: George puns on the meaning of this expression, thus turning the conversation in a way which shows his complete indifference. She means 'what you are doing' (that is, in the 'war' between them). He means 'I have reached page . . . in my book.'

this kick: this act

footwork: manoeuvring. Another metaphor from boxing

the west . . . must eventually . . . fall: a quotation from a characteristically pessimistic choice of reading matter, probably Oswald Spengler's (1880–1936) *Decline of the West* (1922). Albee said of this play that it 'may be all about the decline of the West'

stud: a male horse used for breeding. Here, a virile highly-sexed man

secret little murders: abortions

dry run: a trial run or preliminary attempt

the wave of the future: the new civilisation which George believes Nick represents. He refers to Nick and Martha's flirtation in this way because earlier Nick has admitted that sleeping with the wives of important people is part of his strategy for gaining power and influence

bang: slang for copulate

Act III   pages 109–126

Martha returns to the stage, talking to herself. It appears that Nick has proved too drunk to succeed in making love to her. Nick joins her and she mocks him for his failure. She expresses disgust with herself and her sexual adventures and tells Nick that her husband, despite appearances, is the only man who ever made her happy. Nick doesn't believe her. She regards his disbelief as an indication of his superficiality of outlook. She is, in fact, perfectly sincere in her remarks about George, and the revelation of this fact prepares us for the new understanding that is established at the end of the play. As a reward for his failure she appoints Nick 'houseboy' and sends him, in this capacity, to answer the doorbell when it rings. It is George with some flowers: 'for the dead', he says (in Spanish) but no one notices or takes it up. He embarrasses Nick by pretending to mistake him for his son. Martha and George engage in a more or less meaningless argument, but unite against Nick, humiliating him by discussing and debating his status as 'houseboy'. George proposes a final game, 'Bringing up Baby'. Both Nick and Martha try to dissuade him but George insists and sends Nick to fetch Honey for it. Martha seems surprisingly afraid of the game, but agrees, none the less.

NOTES AND GLOSSARY:

Hump the Hostess! . . . Fat chance: The first indication in Act III that Nick has failed to make love to Martha

Up the spout: *THE POKER NIGHT*: Martha's ruminations do not make sense, but their reference is obviously phallic

affects a brogue: (*stage direction*) assumes an Irish accent

a flop in some departments: a failure in some things (meaning here his sexual performance)

lunk-heads: fools

voyeur: one who prefers watching sex to performing

I don't think he's got a vertebra intact: Martha has threatened to break George's back; Nick believes it is already broken, in other words that he is 'spineless' or 'gutless', lacking in self-assertion

The stallion's mad . . . The gelding's all upset: a stallion is a breeding male horse, a gelding one that has been castrated. Martha is taunting him for his sexual failure

swing wild: another boxing metaphor

Can't you get the latch up, either?: to open the door. Another reference to Nick's sexual failure

houseboy . . . flunky: male servants

gigolo: a male prostitute

Violence: presumably she means 'violets' but as an ingredient in her wedding bouquet 'violence' is very appropriate in view of her behaviour as a wife

hopscotch: a children's game

Chastity: an ironic choice of nickname for Martha

was this after you killed them?: see note on 'something funny in his past', p.32 above

truth and illusion: this theme comes into prominence at this stage in preparation for George's destruction of the 'illusion' or fantasy upon which their marriage has been built

SOOOWWWIIIEEE!!: calling Honey as if she were a mother pig

dip: dipsomaniac or drunkard

slugging: punching. Another boxing metaphor

baby poo: sentimental baby language, used here ironically

Act III   page 127—end

As part of the game proposed by George, Martha gives a long and sentimental account of their 'son's' birth and childhood. As she proceeds, George starts to recite the words of the Requiem Mass of the Roman Catholic church. As this is a service for the dead, it implies that the 'son' is dead, though no one understands at first. Honey interrupts, touched by Martha's account of mothering to say she would like a child – a radical change in her outlook. Martha tries to stop, but George forces her to continue by blaming the 'son's' adult problems on her: she, in turn, blames him. George starts to recite the Requiem again, and in spite of an attempt by Honey to stop the game, announces that the 'son' is dead. It has the desired effect. Martha is furious, saying George has no right to do this. George, however, continues as if the 'son' and his death were real, making it impossible for her in front of the guests to make her point. He forces Honey to confirm that the telegram did arrive. Nick finally understands what the game is about. As Martha continues to protest that George has 'broken the rules' of their game, Nick and Honey leave. Left alone, George and Martha are sobered and apprehensive at the prospect of a life unsupported by illusion.

NOTES AND GLOSSARY:

bassinet: cradle

Absolve, Domine . . . : George begins his recitation of words from the Requiem Mass. He has deliberately chosen a point in Martha's narrative where her sentimentality has reached a climax, thereby making the effect of his 'burial' of the 'son' more brutal and conclusive. There is no connection between the particular sentences of the requiem that George pronounces and the parts of Martha's reminiscence with which they are juxtaposed. Readers with no knowledge of Latin need not, therefore, concern themselves with their exact meaning: it is enough to know that they are connected with the burial of the dead. A full translation is given below. No one at first understands the meaning of George's performance

all truth being relative: that is, there is no such thing as absolute truth. George's scepticism does not, however, prevent him from destroying 'illusion'

I want a child: Martha really enjoys her charade. It is because of her evident feeling for motherhood, even imaginary motherhood, that Honey undergoes this change of heart, and wants babies after having previously aborted them. The change effected in Nick and Honey's marriage is a dramatic prelude to the change that is to be effected in George and Martha's

slashing, braying residue: violent, screaming remains of a human being

harridan: a quarrelsome old woman

You can't do that: Martha means he has no right to 'kill' the 'son'. She keeps saying this, but in front of her guests her words make no sense, because she introduced the subject of her son as if he were real. George and Nick both point this out to her (Act III, p.136), saying that George hasn't the power of life and death. The argument between George and Martha continues at cross purposes like this until Nick finally understands

We **couldn't:** the emphasis on 'we' in George's answer and in Martha's endorsement of it is significant. Albee's stage directions indicate '*a hint of communion*' in their agreement on this point. Up till now the illusion of their child had sustained their relationship: now joint acceptance of their childlessness is to be a bond between them

Who's Afraid of Virginia Woolf: when the song is sung for the final time it bears the meaning 'Who is afraid of a life without illusion?' Albee himself said that this was what the title meant, though it is only here that its meaning becomes apparent

Below is a translation of the words from the Roman Catholic Requiem Mass quoted in Act III. The page references are to the text of the play.

Absolve, Domine, animas omnium fidelium defunctorum ab omni vinculo delictorum: O Lord absolve all the souls of the faithful departed from every chain of their sins (p.129)

Et gratia tua illis succurrente, mereantur evadere judicium ultionis: And with your grace helping them, may they deserve to escape the judgement of vengeance (p.129)

Et lucis aeternae beatitudine perfrui: And to enjoy the blessedness of eternal light (p.129)

In Paradisum deducant te Angeli: May the Angels bear you to Paradise (p.129)

In memoria aeterna erit justus: ab auditione mala non timebit: The just shall be in eternal remembrance: he shall not fear evil tidings (p.130)

Dominus vobiscum: The Lord be with you (p.130)

Libera me, Domine, de morte aeterna, in die illa tremenda: Set me free O Lord from eternal death in that terrible day (p.132)

Quando caeli movendi sunt et terra: When the heavens are to be moved, and the earth (p.132)

Dum veneris judicare saeculum per ignem: When you come to judge this generation by fire (p.132)

Tremens factus sum ego, et timeo, dum discussio venerit, atque ventura ira: I tremble and am afraid when the shaking of all things is at hand and the wrath to come (pp.132–3)

Quando caeli movendi sunt et terra: When the heavens are to be moved, and the earth (p.133)

Dies illa, dies irae, calamitatis et miseriae; dies magna et amara valde: That day, the day of wrath, of calamity and misery, that great and most bitter day (p.133)

Dum veneris judicare saeculum per ignem: When you come to judge this generation by fire (p.133)

Requiem aeternam dona eis, Domine: et lux perpetua luceat eis: Grant them into eternal rest O God: and let light perpetual shine upon them (p.133)

Libera me domine de morte aeterna in die illa tremenda: quando caeli movendi sunt et terra: Set me free O Lord from eternal death on that terrible day: when the heaven and earth are to be moved (p.133)

Dum veneris judicare saeculum per ignem: When you come to judge this generation by fire (p.133)

Kyrie, eleison. Christe, eleison. Kyrie, eleison: Lord, have mercy. Christ, have mercy. Lord, have mercy (pp.133 and 136). (These words are Greek, not Latin, but form part of the Liturgy.)

Part 3

Commentary

Background and setting

Who's Afraid of Virginia Woolf? is set in a small college in the eastern part of the United States. New England, as that area is called, is where the most ancient and prestigious of America's institutions are to be found. Life there has a rooted quality that contrasts with that in the more recently settled parts of the continent. Something of this contrast is apparent in the difference between George and Nick. George represents the old world: weary and disillusioned perhaps, but more formidable in his sophistication than appears on the surface. Nick represents the new world, something of the frontier spirit even: he is dynamic and positive in outlook but his complacent self-confidence is naïve. To the New Englander he is 'bucolic'; he belongs to the fringes of civilisation, not its heart. Though not in the first rank, the college is a distinguished and conservative institution: ivy grows upon its walls even if it does not belong to the so-called Ivy League, which comprises the most ancient and distinguished American universities. Even the disillusioned George admits as much.

Within this milieu the characters themselves are above average: George and Martha because Martha's father is President of the College; Nick and Honey because of Nick's precocious talent. Due weight should be given to this fact. The element of social criticism in the play is enhanced by being directed towards the best that America has to offer by way of civilisation. If such people are seen to be degraded, it is implied, what can society as a whole be like?

Although the play is intensely concentrated upon the four lives as they are affected by the exchanges of the night, it is not lacking in wider references to society as a whole. It is not for nothing that George and Martha are so named after the founder President, George Washington, and his wife; they function in the play to some extent as representatives of the élite, as well as individuals in their own right.

How does the play present the immediate setting, on the one hand, and the wider society on the other? One of the first characteristics presented to us is that it is notably alcoholic, with no distinction between the sexes. For a country with Prohibition only three decades in its past this suggests some disparity between ideal and reality.

With heavy drinking goes a high level of sexual promiscuity.

'Musical beds is the faculty sport round here', George informs Nick. Later he compares the faculty wives on their shopping expeditions in New Carthage to the prostitutes in a South American town. Ambition as well as lust prompts the men to sleep with them. This is an attack not only on the sexual morals of the faculty but also on its professional seriousness. If influence is really achieved in this way, the academic standards of the college are at risk.

You should consider the period in which the play is set. Though written in the early 1960s the play reflects the world of the preceding decade. The Second World War (1939–45) is still a relatively recent memory: George reflects that none of the faculty was killed in the war and sees it as typical of the smugness and decadence of New England that they so successfully avoided danger when civilisation was at stake. It is the period of the Cold War, when in the new power structure resulting from the Second World War, superpowers of the Communist and the free world were in dangerous confrontation. In a drunken and agitated moment George irrelevantly proposes an imaginary alliance with Russia against the Chinese. Fears of totalitarian takeover, deriving from the political anxieties of this period, centre upon Nick and the eugenic Utopia which biologists are supposedly to establish. Nick, as Albee himself intimates, is so named after Nikita Khrushchev, the Soviet leader of the time. His adversary, George, has a representative American name. The confrontation of the old world values of Western civilisation, represented by George the historian, and the Brave New World of Nick the biologist is given a contemporary political dimension by the associations of their names. On a post-Vietnam audience the point might be lost.

The period of the play also pre-dates the era of self-conscious liberation normally associated with the 1960s. Later in that decade the lax morality of the college would have passed without comment: here it is supposed to be shocking, and the outcry the play occasioned shows that it was received as such. Questions concerning the Christian religion are touched upon with some seriousness too: the religious showmanship and profiteering of Nick's father-in-law are seen as discreditable; George asks what his faith was; he himself is familiar with the Roman Catholic liturgy, though it is not clear that he professes the faith. Even Martha expresses anxiety about her atheism. Confrontation between traditional accounts of life's meaning and the negations of existentialism was the mood of members of the avant-garde with whom Albee associated in his apprentice years. Later in the 1960s, this would have appeared very dated and discussion of these matters would have revolved round Eastern sages and gurus. Lastly, the play also pre-dates recent movements for the emancipation of women. It is assumed that careers in the university are pursued by men: Martha's discontent centres upon her husband's lack of achievement, not the frustration of her own. George and Martha's fantasy of a child, and Honey's refusal to have one, lose their point if they are not seen against a background where the sanctity of family life is still assumed, if imperfectly maintained.

Themes

Truth and illusion

The central theme of this play is the necessity, however painful, of the removal of illusion from any relationship. In the play the process is indeed painful and the result uncertain, but it is presented none the less as imperative. It is embodied in the title together with the concluding line. Albee himself spelled out the title as meaning 'Who's afraid of a life without illusion?'. In the life of George and Martha the illusion involved is the fiction that they have a child. This fantasy they indulge to compensate for not only their actual childlessness, but also the unfruitful quality of the conjoint life. This is compounded of professional failure and disillusion on George's part, desultory infidelity on hers, and continual bickering on the part of both of them. Their quarrelling escalates to a point where she breaks their rules by revealing the fiction to strangers as if it were true: this forces him, to his great discomfiture and indignation, to sustain the fiction publicly. He in turn puts an end to it unilaterally by publicly announcing the 'son's' death, which she, correspondingly, is forced to accept. The psychological impact of the circumstances and the manner in which he does this are such that there is no question of the fiction being revived. As a result, they are forced to face their life together as it is, not to take refuge in what it might have been.

For Nick and Honey, too, something of the same kind takes place. The illusion here is their image as a presentable, up-and-coming young couple: the truth is the squalid background to their marriage, that he was trapped into the marriage by her supposed pregnancy and acquiesced in it because of the ill-gotten money she inherited. In addition, their present childlessness is not, as they present it, that of a young couple who have not had time to settle down. It is the result of secret abortions on Honey's part. It is hinted, but never made clear, that the hysterical pregnancy which enforced their marriage was also a real one, secretly terminated by Honey. Nick's total disloyalty to this relationship is also exposed: he is prepared to reveal these secrets to a hostile stranger, and to be unfaithful to her when she is in the same house, with the aim of advancing his career. At the same time he feels at liberty to despise George for his lack of moral fibre. Nick's public discomfiture by the despised George and his failure to make love to Martha destroy his self-complacency. That is the truth that he is forced to face, while Honey comes to terms, apparently, with her reluctance to bear children.

Attention is drawn in the play to the centrality of truth and illusion as a theme by the repetition of those words in a different and more peripheral context. In Act III George has been describing a visit he claims to have made to the Mediterranean. The truth of his account is called in question. Nick loses patience and George refuses to let the argument drop, asking 'Truth and illusion. Who knows the difference...?' Debate ensues concerning Nick's success as Martha's lover. Nick pleads with Martha that she should maintain that he succeeded. She does so, and when George believes her she is disappointed. 'Truth and illusion, George; you don't know the difference.' George answers, 'No; but we must carry on as though we did' (p.119). The debate continues until George loses patience. Martha pleads 'Truth or illusion, George. Doesn't it matter to you...at all?' (p.120). The words are repeated in this way to indicate that this quest is becoming important to them and as a prelude to the moment when George assaults the major illusion of their lives.

Conflict

Another theme of the play is the significance, and the value, even, of conflict. The quarrels in which Martha and George engage are not merely the product of drunkenness and ill-nature. When Nick makes the apparent row between George and Martha a reason for leaving, George explains that they do it for 'exercise'. Martha expresses a similar notion. George in exasperation says 'you can humiliate me, you can tear me apart...and that's perfectly all right...that's O.K.' Martha replies 'You can stand it! You married me for it!' (Act II, p.92). She admits her own enjoyment of the process when, surprisingly, she sings his praises to Nick: 'George...whom I will bite so there's blood' (Act III, p.113). And it is evident, too, in the pleasure they show in each other after some of their rougher encounters. For example, before the arrival of their guests they quarrel fiercely, but twice they pause and laugh, when she says he has no guts and when he says that she is balding. The scare George creates when he pretends to murder her with the fake shotgun clearly gives her pleasure. And again when Martha remonstrates with George for exposing the secrets of Nick and Honey's marriage he replies that he did it for her (Act II, p.91). In this connection it is significant how full the play is of boxing metaphors. Most are employed to describe married life, and many come from Martha, who is surprisingly knowledgeable on the subject.

She knows, for example, what the middleweight limit is (how many male readers do?); and she uses technical phraseology in her account of the boxing incident with George. The boxing incident, and the zest with which she relates it, is highly characteristic, and of symbolic significance.

Conflict in this play, however, is more than the expression of a sado-masochistic relationship between Martha and George in which they engage in violence for the stimulus it provides. George's hostile behaviour to both Nick and Honey does not, in any case, come into this category. Conflict is the purifying flame in which truth and illusion are separated. In the case of George and Martha it is the escalation of their quarrel that precipitates George's decision to end the fantasy of their child. Similarly it is the conflict with Nick that prompts George to elicit Nick's secrets: when the conflict has become fiercer he reveals them. George also probes Honey's secrets and confronts her with his knowledge of her abortions in a fierce bullying manner (Act II, pp.105–6).

The kind of conflict that we see here is quite incompatible with normal good manners and minding one's own business. In the conflict between George and Nick, Nick is forced out of just such a stance of polite detachment. The process is justified when we see how hollow is that politeness of his, and how, beneath it, he is grasping, assertive and unprincipled. In the earlier exchanges between George and Nick it is possible that our sympathies are with the latter: he is attempting what seems to be decent behaviour in the embarrassing situation of a stranger's family quarrel. Nick, the 'bucolic' from the Middle West, appears the civilised one; George, the sophisticated New Englander, appears the barbarian. But when Nick's real character is revealed, we feel he has deserved the treatment he has received from George, his exposure and humiliation. Similarly the usual courtesies of marriage are incompatible with this ruthless quest for reality. Between Nick and Honey these courtesies have not been so totally abandoned as they have by George and Martha. Yet their relationship is empty whereas between George and Martha there is, however obscured, a bedrock of affection and esteem.

Conflict, and the abandonment of good manners in pursuit of reality and contact, formed the substance of *The Zoo Story*. These are themes of enduring interest to Albee. The contact Jerry so dramatically establishes at the end of *The Zoo Story* is also what George aims at with Nick, who throws the words 'contact' and 'communicate' back at him (Act II, p.73).

At the climax of the play, when George is about to announce the death of the fantasy son, he talks of a surgeon's knife penetrating to the marrow (Act III, pp.124–5). Marrow is vital, but hard to get at.

The surgical metaphor implies that its exposure is painful. The implication in this play is that the marrow, the inner core of reality in an individual or a relationship, is worth exposing, however indecorous and painful the process and however unwelcome the result.

Parents and children

In his earlier work Albee's own circumstances affected his work, directing him towards the themes of parenthood, childlessness and adoption. In *The American Dream* the most ferocious impact of the play is connected with this theme. Mommy reveals, in typically surreal manner, that as soon as the adopted child manifested signs of normal, independent life it was progressively mutilated by her husband and herself: other defects of a symbolic kind, like feet of clay and absence of guts, were then detected, and when the child finally died the parents demanded their money back from the adoption society. The confusion of sacred ties with American consumerism could hardly have been pointed more savagely. The subject is obviously one about which Albee felt strongly.

The four characters in *Who's Afraid of Virginia Woolf?* are not part of the steady continuum from generation to generation. We learn that Martha was morbidly attached to her father in a way which has precluded happiness with her husband; of her mother we only learn that her father remarried – whether as a widower or divorcé we are not told. George's parents constitute one of the unsolved mysteries of the play. There is talk of his having killed them in separate accidents, yet his own account attributes their deaths to someone who could not be himself. The introduction of a theme at once so arresting and so irrelevant can only suggest that Albee is excessively preoccupied with family life gone wrong. Yet, unexplained as this theme is, it is at least in harmony with the rest of the play, where family life is generally unsatisfactory. Honey had a father who was, it is hinted, a hypocrite and a crook. No reference is made to Nick's parents. He is associated with eugenic utopias in which parenthood is out of date: we hardly think of Nick as either son or father.

The generation represented on stage is childless. In George and Martha's case this is simply a misfortune. In Nick and Honey's it is by her deliberate choice: we learn that she refuses to be a mother because of the pain. The childlessness of these characters is symbolic of a more generalised unfruitfulness both in their lives as individuals and in society as a whole. George and Martha compensate for their unfruitfulness, he by ineffectual and retrospective intellectualism, she by sexual adventure, both by alcohol and marital conflict. The sterility of Nick and Honey's life consists of her selfishness and his lust for power.

History and biology

The conversations between George and Nick consist mostly of hostile small-talk leading to the exposure of Nick's secrets and his intentions. But one theme is noticeable and stands out amid this process: it centres upon their respective subjects, history and biology. It is given sufficient prominence to justify an examination of the light it throws upon the characters and Albee's intentions as a whole.

It is clear that George is not hostile towards Nick solely on the grounds of his subject, because George is already behaving offensively towards him by the time he learns that his subject is biology. But as soon as he does find out, the scope of his hostility widens. George, without giving Nick a reasonable opportunity to explain his views, launches into an attack on the intentions of biologists. He accuses Nick of intending to set up a utopia of perfect human specimens bred in test tubes such as Huxley described in *Brave New World*. Nick for him becomes the pioneer of the new society, part of the 'wave of the future' as he describes it. As an historian, concerned with the past, he sees himself and Nick as naturally in opposition. He contrasts the respective values of the pioneers of the new age and the guardians of the old. George says he feels threatened by Nick. Of course this partly means that he individually is threatened by Nick, as he is, on a sexual and professional level: the context, however, reveals that he is referring chiefly to the battle between the old and the new as represented by them both.

George, as a historian, is quick to see that Nick is part of a threatening trend. He equates Nick's own ruthlessness with the ruthlessness of the new order he represents. For instance, when he detects that money reconciled Nick to his forced marriage, and Nick asks why he wants to know, he replies 'I'm fascinated by the methodology . . . by the pragmatic accommodation by which you wave-of-the-future boys are going to take over' (Act II, p.68). Marrying for money is part of this 'pragmatic accommodation'. The thrust goes home: Nick is angry and says 'You're starting in again'. He lures Nick into admitting that he proposes to use sex to advance his ambition. Nick is joking, but revealing himself more than he knows (Act II, p.72). Nick's intention is obviously only latent at this stage but it is not long before he tries to fulfil it. George was right in his guess.

As well as feeling threatened by the way the 'wave-of-the-future boys' try to gain power, George detests the kind of civilisation that he expects them to create. Firstly he sees that it will entail a loss of liberty: and the totalitarian aspect of Nick's 'Brave New World' is emphasised by associating him with Khrushchev, a bogey-figure to the average American. George's comment is all the more effective for its understatement. 'There will be a dank side to it, too. A certain amount of regulation will be necessary....' Vivid details of a sterilising operation follow and he concludes, 'there will be a certain ... loss of liberty ... as a result of this experiment' (Act I, p.46). Secondly, in purging society of the physically unfit and controlling the characteristics that will go to make the new breed, George foresees the loss of that diversity of cultures and races which has been his life's study. He is not compensated for this loss by the thought of a world consisting of people like Nick.

The all-American boy with perfect physique and wholly uninteresting mind appears in *The Sandbox* and *The American Dream* and would seem to be an object of Albee's own abhorrence. The possibility that, as well as being a characteristic American type, he really is the wave of the future constitutes a part of the social criticism which features in much of Albee's work. In this play it is not the centre of attention, neither is the opposition between George's history and Nick's biology and what they stand for. Nevertheless, the point is made that the all-American boy with his good looks and physique and his confident pursuit of success is really worthless and unprincipled, now more akin to the totalitarian than to the lover of liberty that every good American supposes himself to be. The future, Albee is saying, could all too easily belong to such people, especially if the guardians of the older order are as demoralised as George. There is all too great a danger that tradition and civilisation could be overturned as mindlessly as Nick rejects George's warning to avoid the 'quicksand' of the unprincipled pursuit of power. George emphasises this in a long speech about civilisation, at the end of which he repeats Nick's words of dismissal 'Up yours' (Act II, pp.73–4). It was after all, a pre-eminently all-American figure, Henry Ford (1863–1947), who pronounced that 'History is bunk'.*

Materialism and success worship

Closely allied to the critique of society implied in Albee's portrayal of Nick is a background of materialism and success worship. Background is the appropriate word, for the centre of the play is not here as it was, for instance in *The American Dream*. But it is undoubtedly present and constitutes a part of that wider reference to society as a whole which is a feature of Albee's work in general and of this play in particular.

The opening of the play sounds the note unmistakably when Martha comes in imitating Bette Davis in a film: the character she imitates is a discontented housewife. She comes in, explains Martha, 'from a hard day at the grocery store'. Very naturally, George supposes that the

* He made the remark in the witness-box in a libel suit against the *Chicago Tribune* in 1919.

character in question to be a shopkeeper. No, explains Martha, 'She's a housewife; she buys things'. That, we understand, is the business of her life, and occupies a whole day. And such is the character Martha chooses in self-parody, to mimic. A dramatist of Albee's skill could not mean nothing by such an opening.

It is on Martha that this theme centres. She embodies American consumerism. Her greedy drinking, the gin dribbling down her chin, the large teeth that crack ice-cubes, the voracity of her sex-life, all add up to a repulsive picture of consumerism run wild. Sex and drink are within her reach, but the attitude affects what is beyond it, too. She would have liked (in most moods) a husband more conspicuously successful. She chides him for breaking a bottle of spirits he can ill afford, referring to the low salary he commands; later she compares him to the promising young men at the party (Act II, p.95). The other thing outside Martha's grasp is, of course, a child. It is not surprising that a character so impatient of opposition should react to such a circumstance in the way she does. Unable to bear a child, she must invent one. No particular emphasis is placed upon this connection: but the main theme of the play, namely this fantasy and its destruction, is made psychologically more convincing by this element in Martha's character.

Her character is evident, too, in her attitude to the college. The value she places upon success within the university is unmistakable in her eager response to Nick, her envious glances at up-and-coming young men at her father's party and her exasperation with her failed husband. But though she values it as a sphere for conspicuous success she has little appreciation of its real value and purpose. This emerges in her complaints about George at the faculty party and her contempt for his academic work. Her notion of the role George was to have played, had he not proved inadequate, seems more appropriate to a tycoon than an academic. The point is made yet more explicit when she says George is 'expected to *be* somebody, not just some nobody, some bookworm, somebody who's so damn . . . contemplative, he can't make anything out of himself . . . ' (Act I, p.57). Thus are reading and thinking, along with writing, dismissed from her concept of the academic life. As in many books about university dons, undergraduates get scarcely a mention: the one mention they do get is George's advice to Martha to 'keep her paws clean for the undergraduates'. George's account of the faculty wives on their shopping expeditions suggests that she is not exceptional: she is in any case a recognisable American type.

Success worship in the play centres more, however, on the character of Nick, and this is treated more fully in the previous section 'History and Biology' and in the analysis of his character below. But it is worth noticing here how the two women react to his athletic achievements and precocious academic distinction. Honey's simpering modesty and Martha's eager flattery are matched by his own self-complacency. George alone is unimpressed, calling him a smug son of a bitch. But even he is unable to ignore Nick's distinctions, and feels uncomfortable and threatened by them.

There is enough in this portrayal of American society to show that Albee has seen and deplored its materialism and success worship; but the emphasis of the play is not here. A point is made, however, in the distribution of attention. A couple with no great future ahead of them, but who have consciously faced up to the truths of their relationship and their destiny, are accorded prime significance; while Nick and Honey, who could in the end be far more evidently successful and influential but have merely had the truth thrust upon them, are given second place. This for Albee is what makes a couple, whose future is mediocre by ordinary American standards, worthy of our interest, while the promising one, Nick, is dismissed.

The characters

George

Our knowledge of George's life before the action of the play begins consists partly of an unresolved mystery concerning his adolescence and partly of the circumstances of his marriage and early career.

The unresolved mystery has to do with his parents. In the course of a conversation with Nick he tells a long story dating from his schooldays (Act II, p.61). In this he speaks of a character who had killed his mother with a shotgun. Nick enquires what happened to the boy and George replies that the following year he drove a car into a tree, killing his father, and that he was moved from the hospital to an asylum where he had been completely silent for thirty years. The end of the story, which is told with considerable dramatic emphasis, quite clearly could not apply to George. However, when Martha exposes him in front of Nick by telling the story of his novel and his failure to publish it, she equates the subject of the story, namely the boy who killed his parents, with George. She refers to 'something funny in his past' (Act II, p.81). George's anger rises when he anticipates the revelation that the boy had killed his father and mother to an extent which at least suggests it could be him. The climax of her mockery comes when George is said to have claimed the novel was autobiographical. However, even this is ambiguous, since it could perfectly well act as a description of the story as George had told it to Nick, without George as the accidental killer but as a member of the same party. Again George's anger could be thought disproportionate to a revelation consisting only of his humiliation at the hands of his father-in-law. Elsewhere Martha says 'Before I'm through with you, you'll wish you'd died in that automobile, you bastard' (Act II, p.93). This again suggests that it was George who has been the killer, but again it remains inconclusive. The last piece of evidence occurs when George claims that his parents had sent him to the Mediterranean as a college graduation present. Nick asks if this was after he had killed them, suggesting that he has taken Martha to mean that George had done so and that he has rejected George's own account of the incident. George refuses to answer, saying only 'Maybe' and Martha says 'Maybe not, too'. This particular conversation ends with the refrain 'Truth and illusion, who knows the difference?' (Act III, pp.118−19).

It seems odd of Albee to introduce an issue of such potential significance and then to leave it unresolved. If those misfortunes had really happened to George they could be seen as contributory factors in his present apathy. On the other hand, brazen though she is, Martha could hardly make it a subject of gleeful mockery. And if this never happened to George at all, what purpose does its introduction serve?

With George's marriage and early career, however, we are on uncontroversial ground. Martha gives an account of it which he does not deny and which his own account to Nick endorses. We learn that Martha, in deference to what she supposed were her father's wishes, conceived the idea of marrying someone who would take over from her father as president. With this idea in mind she looked around among the new recruits to the teaching staff and fell in love with George. She discussed her plan with her father, who approved, until, after two years of this marriage, he decided that George was unsuited to such a position. This embittered Martha against George. Furthermore, their hopes of a child were disappointed.

The opening of the play shows George and Martha as combatants, but with George taking the defensive role. Though she gives more energy to these encounters his rearguard action is made effective by a quick and urbane wit. Though this might suggest that he is reluctant to enter the fray, it is soon made clear that this is not so: enjoyment of their domestic warfare is mutual. This is evident when between rounds, as it were, they show pleasure in each other's company and performance. Yet their quarrelling expresses real discontent on the part of them both; the enjoyment it gives them is a bitter one. When Martha taunts George for his failure, he tacitly admits it and becomes increasingly negative and reclusive. His bookishness takes a pessimistic and sceptical turn: when we see him pick up a book it concerns the inevitable decline of the West, and the only time he expresses certainty it is in what he knows to be an illusion (see Act I, p.49).

George's complaints about the dominance of his father-in-law are ineffectual: he grumbles and denigrates the man in his absence, but does as he is told. He is candid about the emasculating effect of his position as son-in-law to the president: in this, too, he exasperates Martha. It is clear, though, that beneath the exterior of cynical disillusionment with his career and his marriage George has a tenderer side: the part of him that finds satisfaction in the fantasy of a child. We see, however, that this is not an adequate counterbalance to the bad side of his marriage, because even into this fantasy he, like Martha, imports quarrelling and recriminations. He accuses Martha, for example, of sexually assaulting the boy. But there is no evidence that this recrimination is habitual: more likely it is one of the signs that the marriage is undergoing strains so great that the fantasy cannot save it. Certainly his determination to keep it secret suggests that it means much to him.

In confrontation with Nick, George shows not only a more aggressive, but an altogether more formidable side. On the one hand Nick appears to put him at a disadvantage, and yet, on the other, how cleverly he turns the tables on Nick. Confrontation of this kind is the essence of their relations from the start: not only because George is blatantly rude to his unwanted guests and makes no attempt to modify his quarrel in their presence, but also because of the unmistakable contrast they present. Nick is full of complacent self-confidence: his good looks, his physique, his promising career giving him an obvious advantage over the ageing and unsuccessful George. Furthermore, George will be well aware that Martha has invited them home because she finds Nick attractive (Act I, p.14). The reception Nick gets is not calculated to alter his impression that George is beneath his attention. His frigid politeness makes that quite clear, and he is determined to leave as soon as his wife returns to the living room. George is just polite enough to prevent this happening by offering drinks at appropriate moments, but otherwise he employs a thoroughly impolite range of tricks to break through Nick's façade of dignified reserve, and to disconcert him by abrupt changes of subject, ignoring what Nick says, throwing his words back at him, pausing, changing tone and pace. This aggression is mixed with odd manifestations of inferiority: he compares his physique with Nick's and accords it a pathetic accolade, and he offers to play handball with Nick when Nick says he doesn't play very well. But mostly he shows himself a skilful and remorseless needler.

At the beginning of Act II this skill is manifested in eliciting Nick's confidences concerning his marriage. When Nick's account shows signs of flagging he embarks on his own (Act II, p.66). He confesses the motive for his curiosity quite truthfully but in a jocular way that prevents him being taken seriously. He does this twice. He explains that he is interested in Nick's wife's money as part of Nick's strategy for taking over. (Act II, p.68) And again, he admits he is only interested in Nick's life because he wants to 'get the goods' on him (Act II, p.70). He allows Nick to parody himself in an account of how he will rise to power, sleeping with the 'pertinent' wives and so on. He then confronts him with the fact that it is more than parody, and when Nick rejects his warning he has his revenge. Again, the skill and the ruthlessness with which he turns all Nick's confidences back upon him in front of the others, including Honey, shows a surprising steeliness of character. The urbane New Englander is shown to be quite as formidable in his own way as the pushful mid-Westerner. George's contempt for Martha's seduction of Nick robs it of any triumph; and when it fails, Nick's defeat at George's hands is total.

The same steeliness is seen in George's total contempt for Honey. Partly he is ill-disposed towards her because his guests are unwanted anyway; but her silliness confirms his antipathy. At the moment of her entry he rudely mimics her giggle. When dancing is proposed, he offers himself as a partner with calculated grossness, calling her 'sexy', 'angel-tits' and 'monkey-nipples'. But mostly this is because he can hardly see her as a rational, conversible human being, so silly and so drunk is she. However there is one issue on which he confronts her quite seriously, and this is over the matter of her childlessness. He is obsessed with her child-bearing potential, harping continually upon her slim hips. When she proposes leaving he asks her nastily if she is keeping the babysitter up (Act I, p.34). When her sleep-talking reveals that her childlessness is deliberate he reacts very strongly, first with compassion, then with violence, accusing her of secret murders (Act II, pp.105–6). Later, as he tries, unsuccessfully, to make her aware that her husband is making love to Martha, he taxes her again with her refusal to have children.

This ferocity is the obverse of his tenderness towards the family life he has been unable to create. He considers the sordid scene being enacted at that moment, to which childlessness has reduced his own family life, and is indignant that anyone who had the opportunity to do better should reject it. This tenderness towards the possibilities of family life is unexpectedly revealed to be at the heart of George and Martha's relationship. Martha tells the incredulous Nick that George is the only man in her life who has made her happy (Act III, p.113). It is also evidenced in the strength which enables him to lead them into the uncertainties of their new life without illusion in the closing scene.

Critics have seen George as an outsider who has compromised. He adopts something of this when he acts as the main catalyst in the exposure of truth and the destruction of illusion. But he is not, for example, Jerry in *The Zoo Story*, in search of existential truth in a meaningless universe. He acts in the service of traditional values: order, decency, the family, even religion. He is the well-disguised spokesman of Albee's own conservatism.

Martha

Our knowledge of Martha's life before the play begins derives from her own account of it. We learn of her exceptional closeness to her father, her abortive first marriage and its annulment, her courtship of George and her subsequent disappointment in him. This disappointment is the immediate purpose of her narrative; the contrast with her father, and the role she and her father had planned for George being a part of it. Her week-long marriage to the lawn-mower has no bearing upon the humiliation of George, but it contributes to the whole picture of her hardness and cynicism about sex. The brazen manner in which she speaks of the event is characteristic (Act I, pp.52–3). The subsequent period as her father's hostess cemented her attachment to him in a way which is to prove a barrier to her happiness in marriage.

This background gives psychological credibility to the kind of relationship she has with George. She is by nature loud, dynamic and voracious; George is reclusive and intellectual. This difference of temperament is not of itself an obstacle to their happiness. However, allied to the disappointment of their childlessness and the failure of his career, it has driven her to heavy drinking, promiscuity and general abandon, which arouses in him distaste and contempt while giving her no real satisfaction. She disgusts herself, she says (Act III, p.111).

Their real hostility to each other, then, has been turned into a bitter, sado-masochistic game to sustain and enliven their relationship. Though Martha is, if anything, the more eager participant in this game, in moments of self-knowledge she can see that it is destructive of what few chances of real happiness remain. Thus her account of the boxing match, which is symbolic of this aspect of their relationship, expresses an ambiguous feeling towards the incident. On the surface she tells it with eager enthusiasm to bait George. But as the account progresses the misgivings – already evident in her insistence that it was an accident – predominate. '*Rueful*' in the stage directions is the key word, expressing the regret that accompanies her relish. But her discontented, aggressive self finally supervenes. 'It's an excuse anyway', she says (Act I, p.40). The same ambiguous note is sounded after the fiasco with Nick when she declares that George is the only one who has made her happy, and adds with unusual candour and self-knowledge that she herself destroys her happiness by rejecting him (Act III, p.113). She is aware of this ambiguity: the discontent that refuses what it wants, and the relish of cruelty on the one hand, and on the other the wistful regret and appreciation. And she concludes that one day she will go too far.

This passage, which is addressed to Nick, is suggestive of her more tender side: the side which cherishes the fantasy of the child, and which enables her to put on such a convincing performance that Honey is converted to the idea of maternity by her account of it. It represents Martha on the verge of the change which it requires George's announcement to complete. To this change, her humility and self-knowledge are the prelude. But though they represent one aspect, they are not typical of her relations with him during the main body of the play, or of her nature as it is characteristically manifested.

With Nick her unregenerate self is seen very clearly. Nick at first is a convenient weapon in her warfare with George. Inviting guests at that hour, we understand, is a provocation in itself, her zest for parties exceeding his. Nick's physical attractions, which she admits, are made a further provocation. In addition the invitation enables her to assert her father's will over George's. For Nick she dresses up seductively: an act which vexes George considerably. She then draws Nick out on the subject of his academic and athletic achievements, flattering him and ogling him, at the same time not permitting George to ignore what constitutes a painful contrast with himself:

> MARTHA (*with great enthusiasm*): BOXING! You hear that, George?
> GEORGE: (*resignedly*): Yes, Martha.
>
> (Act I, p.37)

George is 'resigned', presumably, to an indulgence of her relish of violence, of the male physique, and of the humiliating incident where she knocked him down. Each of these she pursues with characteristically eager indecency. Other ways in which she uses Nick in her campaign against George are to take Nick's side in the debate about biology and history and to make Nick the audience for her chronicle of George's failure. The crowning provocation is, of course, her seduction of Nick. She certainly had initiated the flirtation but responsibility for its conclusion rests partly with George for refusing to intervene. Nick's self-complacency prevents him from seeing more in the situation than what seems to him a natural preference for himself over George. The subtleties of Martha's desire for George to drop his indifference and save her from herself pass Nick by, as does the extent to which he is simply being used by her. Martha also sees clearly that Nick's motives are those he had expressed to George: to increase his influence by getting 'the biggest goose in the gangle' as he calls her.

Martha's well practised control of this situation makes her a formidable adversary when he disappoints her as a lover. In this scene we see her at her most destructive, and, since Nick has betrayed himself so completely, we relish the spectacle. The coarse realism with which she harps upon the physical details of his failure, the foul-mouthed repartee with which she blasts away the dignity behind which he still attempts to hide, the alliance with George against him, all show her at her violent best. Also it is an improvement in her to find a more fitting victim than George, and this prepares us for her new self to emerge.

It should, of course, be remembered that the 'new Martha' belongs to the suppositious future and is outside the play. The Martha we see up to the end is for the most part the only one presented to our view. This character is delineated not only by her behaviour on stage, and indeed her own account of it, but by metaphor. On her first appearance it is she herself who introduces the comparison with a discontented housewife, the business of whose life is shopping. It is from George that most of the metaphors connected with monsters and wild animals come, while the other characteristic metaphor, that of boxing, comes from both. The extravagance of her abandon is emphasised in George's picture of half-empty glasses left everywhere, the large teeth that crunch ice-cubes, the dress raised over her head (a theme she herself takes up from George), and the sub-human ferocity of her braying voice. These images, corroborating her actual demeanour on stage, give an unforgettable picture of the personality that has come all but completely to dominate her nature, and which only the violent catharsis of the conclusion can subdue.

Nick

George and Martha are characters whose faults are in the foreground and whose virtues are all but concealed. It takes the traumatic events of the night to reverse this situation so that their relationship might be rebuilt upon the real but obscured strengths of their respective characters. Nick, by contrast, has all his goods in the shop window: for him the events of the night serve only to expose his true character. There is no suggestion that he is improved by the process: he is exposed merely, though in a manner which we cannot but feel is good for him.

On the level of appearances, however, Nick is presented to us as a promising young man; somewhat incongruously mated, perhaps, but otherwise extremely presentable. Morally he has the advantage over George and Martha in that he behaves tactfully in the face of George's unwelcoming behaviour and the embarrassment of his hosts' quarrel. He is modest about his achievements as an athlete and as an academic. He is capable of considerable patience and tact in the face of his wife's gauche and embarrassing behaviour. From time to time he shows himself chivalrously protective towards her. Though he shows the deference due to senior colleagues in his dealings with George, he does not meet aggression with weakness and will defend himself where necessary. Martha's initial advances he demurs at without embarrassment or prudery. Altogether, we feel, a young man who will go far.

The course of the play, however, steadily reveals what lies behind this façade. Bit by bit his pretensions are exposed: yet surprisingly, as each is manifestly belied, his habits of self-satisfaction remain. Long after matters have progressed beyond the sphere of social correctness and polite non-commitment he continues to deal in them as though they were still appropriate. Even at the play's melodramatic conclusion, with its potent atmosphere of new-found honesty, there is no indication before his dismissal that he has penetrated below the surface of things. It is a part of the comic tradition that the better characters are changed and improved as the play moves from complication to dénouement: the villain, however, survives the conclusion unrepentant and unimproved. This is the contrast between Nick and his hosts; to some extent also between Nick and his wife.

The contrast between Nick's words and his real meaning is continually emphasised in the stage directions. These not only indicate the tone of his replies, but, by way of more exact definition, the motive and feeling that lie behind them. In the moments after his arrival when the four characters are all together his insincerity is manifest. This sets the pattern for behaviour which continues throughout the play.

Nick's tact in the face of his hosts' quarrels is not so much a matter of good breeding as a habit of non-involvement. This habit is reinforced when, as in the present case, the involvement would be with a failed colleague. With his instinct for advancement he has soon put George in this category: with Martha it is noticeable that he is less detached. Further it is presented to us as a defective habit of mind, typical of the scientist. Non-involvement is the recurring theme of his conversation, taken up and thrown back at him by George. For example, when he is first left alone with George, and is thinking of leaving because of the row that is in progress, he makes it his excuse (Act I, p.27). When George and Martha debate the paternity of their 'son' he tries to avert the subject. After Martha has humiliated George and the two men are left alone together, George supplies the word for him as an excuse for not discussing the subject further:

GEORGE: . . . It gets pretty bouncy around here sometimes.
NICK: (*coolly*): Yes . . . I'm sure.
GEORGE: Well, you saw an example of it.
NICK: I try not to . . .
GEORGE: Get involved? Um? Isn't that right?
NICK: Yes . . . that's right.

(Act II, p.58)

In the course of the same scene Nick reacts the same way to George's attempt at explanation. George accuses him of ignoring life in order to preserve his scientific detachment (Act II, p.64). Scientific detachment is equated with lack of human understanding in the later dialogue where Martha tells Nick why George is superior to him (Act III, pp.113 and 114). Thus the events of the play, in making Nick's non-involvement an appropriate response, expose the complacency, egoism and narrowness of mind which lie behind it.

Closely allied to Nick's detachment are the modesty and deference which give to his demeanour a well-bred air. But it is easy to see their hollowness. It takes very little to flush out their exact opposites. He soon sees that he will lose no ground with Martha by denigrating her husband: the trappings of politeness ('Sir?') are rapidly dropped. The old-fashioned respect for seniors implied in his pronouncement 'I have never hit an older man' is, in the context, decidedly back-handed. As he is drawn into the violence of the evening he takes less trouble to hide his sense of his own superiority. At the beginning he remonstrates modestly with Honey when she reveals his athletic and academic achievements. However, reference in the stage instructions to *'a small smile'* and *'that small smile'* indicate that his modesty is a sham, though at this stage he keeps his conceit to himself. Soon he is claiming superiority to George quite openly: 'Don't try to put me in the same class with you.' He is quite sincerely overcome with laughter at the suggestion that George, of all people, could usefully offer him advice. 'Good advice! From you? Oh boy!' he says, and concludes 'You just tend to your knitting, grandma . . . . I'll be O.K.' (Act II, pp.72–3). Finally, secure in Martha's seductive flattery, he openly jeers with her at George while he dances with her: 'He will not be made mock of, for Christ's sake' (Act II, p.83). When George robs him of the triumph of his imminent affair with Martha by expressing indifference, he claims moral superiority: 'I have no respect for you' (Act II, p.103). Afterwards he is still claiming it, this time over both of them. Martha says 'Relax; sink into it; you're no better than anybody else' and he replies 'I think I am' (Act III, p.111). Later he dismisses them as 'kids' (Act III, p.116).

Probably the most complete exposure of Nick's pretensions is in his behaviour towards Honey. She must be something of a liability to someone who wishes to cut an impressive figure in public. His dignity demands, however, that he should behave in a chivalrous manner towards her, however embarrassing her absurdities. That he achieves a measure of success in this is evidenced by George's comment in the middle of his 'Get the Guests' performance: 'he had this mouse, of whom he was solicitous to a point that faileth human understanding . . . given that she was sort of a simp, in the long run . . . .' (Act III, p.88). But the strain tells, and we see Nick losing patience early in the play. Again, the stage directions indicate that his feelings are at odds with his actual words. For instance, when she remonstrates with him for his indecent language, the incident (Act I, p.47) itself emphasises how spurious his chivalry is, because earlier he had objected to George's use of obscene language in front of his wife (Act I, p.34). When Honey announces that she has no sense of humour he reassures her, half-heartedly, with a cliché: 'Yes you have, honey. A quiet one.'

By far the most extreme instance of his hypocrisy, however, is his total betrayal of Honey. He tells the story of their marriage: the absence of any passion, the influence of her money and the fake pregnancy that precipitated it. He does so in coarse and heartless language, and to a man he despises. It is therefore remarkable that, just before George retells the story, he should once more act the chivalrous husband. 'What did you call my wife?' he asks George, who has just addressed her as 'angel-tits'. But Martha's attractions prevent him from pursuing the point. And when he is on the point of making love with Martha he reveals Honey's frigidity.

Both these acts of betrayal backfire on him. George reveals that he knows about the marriage in a manner that resoundingly gives the lie to any pretensions of decency that he may have made. Nick's protestations to Honey inevitably fall very flat at this point, and his censure of George's conduct, however justifiable, is neutralised by his own culpability. It is significant, though, that his crowning accusation is that George's behaviour is damaging, not, as might be expected, to Honey, but to himself (Act II, p.90). His egoism is displayed here in all its shamelessness. His failure to make love to Martha destroys his pretensions to superior masculinity, and his humiliation is intensified by the overt nature of his rivalry with George. Not only does he suffer the indignity of a post-mortem on his failure, but he is made to hear Martha's praises of her husband. In the face of this intolerable situation he remains remarkably thick-skinned. He offers excuses which merely increase his ignominy:

> NICK: You should try me sometime when we haven't been drinking for ten hours and maybe . . .
> MARTHA: (*still braying*): I wasn't talking about your potential; I was talking about your goddamn performance.
>
> (Act III, p.111)

To her protestations of her husband's superiority Nick reacts with stark disbelief (Act III, p.112). The suggestion that his superficiality prevents him believing her, he refuses to entertain. 'I know when a man's had his back broken; I can see that' (Act III, p.114). Yet he is unable to see the extent to which his own back is broken, even when he is forced to beg Martha to lie about his success as a lover. Even at this point he attempts the role of chivalrous protector: 'Do you want me to ... do something to him?' (Act III, p.120). But even for one whose egoism is as invulnerable as his, there is no question of his insisting on chivalrous protection of his wife:

> GEORGE (*Hog-calls towards the hall*): SOOOWWWIIIEEE!! SOOOWWWIIIEEE!!
>
> NICK (*as MARTHA giggles nervously*): Cut that!
>
> GEORGE (*swinging around, facing him*): Then get your butt out of that chair and bring the little dip back in here. (*As NICK does not move*) Now be a good puppy. Fetch, good puppy, go fetch.
>
> (*NICK rises, opens his mouth to say something, thinks better of it, exits.*)
>
> (Act III, p.121)

The final game, 'Bringing up Baby', removes the focus of attention from Nick. One last attempt at self-assertion is decisively quashed, when he tries to prevent the game. George overrules him, and Martha's recitation proceeds (Act III, pp.126–7).

In the conflict between George and Nick, then, the honours are unmistakably with George, as even Nick finally recognises. There is more to Nick's defeat, however, than the defeat of an individual. It has been observed elsewhere that both he and George are representative figures. Nick is a scientist, George an arts man at a time when the division between the 'two cultures' was much emphasised, the scientist being shown to be inept in that human understanding which is supposedly the arts man's special province. Nick is a totalitarian, 'the wave of the future', who proposes to carry all before him; George, the liberal who will conserve the accumulated complexities which civilisation inherits from the past. Nick is a mid-Westerner from a young vigorous civilisation, George a New Englander, decadent and played out on the surface but with the subtleties of an older civilisation in his favour. In the conflict and its result, then, the values of the play and probably Albee's own, are to be found.

Honey

The fact that the play concerns the interaction of two married couples gives Honey's character an importance which in itself it would lack. It is as a couple that Nick and Honey act as catalyst to the transformation which George and Martha undergo, and as a couple they complete the symmetry of the play. However, her character as an individual is developed less fully than those of the other three, for a number of reasons. Firstly, her portrayal is something of a caricature, and as such invites less exploration. Silliness such as hers gives scope for lively dramatic presentation, but does not provide substance for profound analysis. Furthermore, this silliness makes her less conversable than either her highly articulate host and hostess or her husband. In addition the drunkenness which releases the other characters, making them more voluble and less inhibited in their behaviour, removes her from the stage. She is off stage more than any other character, and while she is on stage she is isolated from the others by her failure to understand what is going on around her. This prevents her from being drawn into the kind of conflict which serves to reveal the other characters in depth.

Of her background we learn from Nick that she was the daughter of an evangelist whose dubious activities had left him very rich. She and Nick had been childhood friends and had grown up with their respective families assuming that they would get married. The relationship continued into maturity when it became a fully sexual, albeit relatively passionless one. Honey appeared to become pregnant with the result that Nick was obliged to marry her, only to discover that the 'pregnancy' was a false, hysterical one. Nick was nevertheless content with a marriage that made him rich. In the course of the play when waking from a drunken sleep she seems to reveal that she has, in fact, been secretly aborting. George, at all events, interprets her words so, and accuses her of 'secret little murders'. She reacts hysterically, but does not deny the charge. Before she appears on stage Honey is described by Martha as 'a mousey little type without any hips or anything'. This theme is taken up in conversation by George and Nick when the epithet both use is 'slim-hipped'. The emphasis on this aspect of her physique associates her with the ideas of sexlessness and infertility. Both couples thus contribute to the theme of childlessness in the play; George and Martha through misfortune, Nick and Honey through the latter's choice. It is in the matter of childlessness that the parallel between the couples is worked out; Martha abandoning the pretence that she has a child, Honey that she cannot have one.

Honey's sexlessness and refusal to have a child are psychologically of a piece with her other qualities. George certainly appears to think so when she discloses the truth about herself: 'I should have known...the headaches...the whining...the...' Her infantile manner, her silly demureness, her inability to relate to the adult world as well as her drunkenness are facets of a refusal to fulfil her natural destiny. The focus of the play is not here; but it is worth observing that these qualities, which provide some of the play's most striking comic effects, add up to a psychologically convincing portrayal.

The comic effects Honey provides derive chiefly from her social unawareness. She consistently fails to see the point of what the other characters are saying. This underlines, for example, her futile attempts to save the situation when it is clear that they have arrived in the middle of a quarrel. She appears not to notice George's rude mimicry of her giggle, reacting with stupidly gushing approval of everything in the house. The party, the party song, Martha's father, all receive her exaggerated applause. In the face of George's unrestrained rudeness this is an absurd response. Her unawareness increases as the other characters become absorbed in their quarrels and she becomes drunker. It makes her reactions ludicrously inappropriate. For example, when Martha taunts George with Nick's precocious academic success, she misses the fierce irony of his reply, taking his words at face value (Act I, p.36). Again, when George parodies the genetic utopia he supposes Nick to be planning, she misses the heavy irony. Moreover she fails to see that Martha, in reacting approvingly, is deliberately provoking George. In following Martha she is taking sides in the quarrel, but is quite unaware of it (Act I, p.45).

Further examples can be given. For instance, she seems unaware of the fierce hostility in the debate about the 'son's' return (Act I, p.48). The most striking and effective example, however, occurs in Act II when she fails to recognise herself in George's account of the plot of his pretended second novel. She insists on George continuing when Nick tries to prevent him. She misses all the clues in the introduction: the husband blond, thirty and a scientist, the wife brandy-drinking, the sexual explorations of childhood as well as the significance of Nick's angry response – all pass her by. 'I want to hear the story,' she says simply, 'I love stories.' Gradually she starts to pick up the hints, such as the reference to her father's evangelistic activities and his wealth, saying 'This is familiar' and 'I've heard this story before.' The damaging incidents continue to pour out until she begins, ineffectually, to say 'I don't like this story.' The fact that Nick is trying in every way to prevent the recital that she so ill-advisedly encourages gives an edge to the comedy at this point (Act II, pp.86–9).

Another comic effect is achieved by the contrast between her generally demure manner and her occasional lapses from it. She is too demure to ask plainly where the lavatory is, hesitating and taking refuge in euphemisms in a way which George openly mocks (Act I, p.24). When Nick uses coarse language, she reacts with exaggerated shock, putting her hands over her ears. But shortly after this she quite unnecessarily takes up the word 'bugger' from George when discussing the arrival of the latter's 'son' (Act I, p.48). And when, in Act II, she returns from her bout of vomiting she takes up the cry of 'Hump the Hostess!' with abandon. Again, she shakes her head and tut-tuts at the story of George and Martha's boxing match (Act I, p.40); she overreacts when George pretends to shoot Martha with the parasol-gun

(Act I, p.41), yet when scuffles break out over Martha's account of George's novel she yells 'Violence! Violence!' with indecent excitement, and is disappointed when it comes to an end. Of course, her alternate brandy-drinking and vomiting render this demureness ludicrous. The incongruity of this is deliberately exploited as is her ridiculous pride in the frequency of her vomiting (Act II, p.74).

Another comic effect is the exasperation she arouses in Nick. In spite of the dismal realities of their marriage, they present the appearance of a promising young couple. Her gaucherie, however, constantly puts this appearance at risk. As with the other comic effects she makes possible, this becomes more pronounced as the evening becomes wilder, reaching a climax in Act III. At this point the indignities of which Nick is now victim are considerable: he has revealed the secrets of their marriage, his disloyalty in doing so has been exposed in front of Honey, he has betrayed her by allowing Martha to seduce him yet he has failed sexually. Now he is forced to act the part of a solicitous husband caring for a sick wife. Painful as this undignified pretence must be, it is made infinitely worse by the ridiculous behaviour George mischievously encourages by keeping her repeating the words 'Bunny', 'funny' and her name (Act III, p.128).

This last quotation provides an example of the other effect to which she contributes. This is the way the combined effects of her drunkenness and simplicity cause her to repeat words and phrases of the other speakers, making the dialogue circular – a stylistic feature of Albee's handling of dialogue in the play which is not confined to Honey. It is, however, particularly suited to her character and style.

These are some of the ways in which Albee exploits the comic potential of a necessary but relatively minor character. Honey contributes to the theme of appearance and reality (or 'truth and illusion' in the words of the play) in that, in spite of the endearments she and her husband bandy to and fro, their marriage is loveless and sterile. When this has been exposed, her decision, if it is to be so understood, to have children represents a change wrought by conflict to parallel the change wrought in Martha. In this respect she is contrasted with Nick, who is exposed for what he is, but apparently undergoes no change. That she is more in tune with the play's cathartic conclusion is suggested by her pronouncing 'Amen' to George's 'Requiescat in pace' and her completing the prayer for the dead with the words 'et lux perpetua luceat eis' (Act III, p.138.) By contrast, Nick's attempt on leaving to make some final pronouncement on the night's proceedings is quashed. 'I'd like to . . . ' he begins but George says 'Good night', not allowing him to finish. It is fitting that she should receive more merciful treatment at the end of the play than her husband, for he is seen as an instigator of some of the more malignant trends in American society, whereas she, with her appalling father and yet more appalling husband, is seen as a product of it, or even as a victim.

Structure

Being concerned with characters who have been drinking, and continue to drink, heavily, the play inevitably gives a first impression of disorder and shapelessness. Its action consists largely of talk, albeit interspersed with incidents of random violence, and the talk is often inconsequent and circular as the talk of drunken people generally is. But the play is, in fact, a tightly constructed and concentrated piece, because a number of factors combine to impose shape and structure upon this potentially formless material.

The first of these is that the play observes the unities of time, place and action. The play begins at two o'clock in the morning, and ends before dawn: a period scarcely longer than the duration of the actual play. The scene never moves outside the living room in George's house. And the action centres upon a single theme, namely the destruction of the false basis upon which George and Martha have built their lives. In spite of its apparent randomness, the quarrelling of which the play largely consists is directed to this end.

Albee draws attention to this unity of action by the titles he gives to the acts. These titles point to the progress of the action as it relates to this one central theme. The 'Fun and Games' of Act I raise the ghosts which walk on 'Walpurgisnacht' in Act II and which are finally laid in the 'Exorcism' of Act III, but it is not merely the pretence of a son which is 'exorcised' but a whole habit of life in which the reality is evaded by games and pretences. For all the quarrels of the evening, which appear so dangerously real to an audience and are seen by George and Martha as 'fun and games', are devised by Albee to lead up to the moment when George brings them to an end by the 'exorcism'.

Another device which makes the unity of action manifest, and which serves to alert the audience to the connection between what would otherwise appear random events, occurs in Act II. At this point, Martha has just humiliated George in front of the guests by her account of his second novel. By making George give a name ('Humiliate the Host') to what has just passed, and by making him anticipate the subsequent course of the action by proposing 'Hump the Hostess' and 'Get the Guests', Albee emphasises the shape and direction of the action. The connection between the events to which these names have been given is easier to see: Martha's humiliation of George in front of Nick and her increasing flirtation with the latter are together part of her warfare against George; George's humiliation of Nick is his counter-attack. Naming the games also serves to give prominence to the climax of the play, which is named as a fourth game, 'Bringing up Baby', and makes clearer the point that it is the game that brings game-playing to an end.

Control of climax is another aspect of the deliberate way in which the play is constructed. The confrontations between George and Martha become increasingly violent; when she taunts him with the tale of their 'boxing match', he takes his revenge by pretending to shoot her with the fake gun. The violence in this case is a pretence (Act I, p.41). It is real, though not directed at any person, when George smashes a bottle to stop Martha's recital of their marriage and his failure in the University (Act I, p.56). Real personal violence erupts in their third major row, when he responds to her account of his novel by seizing her throat and has to be fought off by Nick (Act II, p.76).

There is a parallel progression in the stages by which their relationship eventually reaches a deadlock. Though less dramatic, these occasions are more serious in their implications because they affect the foundations of their marriage, not merely the mood of the moment as do the overtly violent occasions described above. This progression begins with George's first sexual rejection of her (Act I, p.17), moves through her mention of the child, which, we are led to understand, is a serious act of war on her part (Act I, p.33); her dressing up, which indicates her intention to flirt with Nick (Act I, p.33); his second rejection of her (Act I, p.42); up to the point where she, uncharacteristically, refuses to appreciate his success in 'Get the Guests', which George says, was all for her (Act II, p.91). This last is the prelude to an argument in which game-playing has no part and in which they admit the deadlock their relationship has reached:

> GEORGE: . . . There is no moment . . . there is no moment any more when we could . . . come together.
> MARTHA (*armed again*): Well, maybe you're right, baby.
> (Act II, p.95)

This mutual admission leads to a declaration of what they call 'total war'. In Martha's case this takes the form of pursuing her flirtation with Nick to its conclusion; in George's by reacting to her behaviour with studied indifference (Act II, pp.103–4).

Act II, then, ends at a point where outrage can go no further. Short-term, surface violence reaches a point where actual physical scuffling breaks out. The other, more serious kind of long-term destructiveness reaches its peak when Martha goes off to bed with Nick, while George refuses, in apparent indifference, to prevent her. No further progression along these lines is dramatically feasible: thus the conclusion of Act II is a kind of false climax, which has the effect of emphasising the radically different nature of the real climax of Act III. The momentousness of George's announcement is prepared for in this way, and also the elaborate build-up to the moment when he makes it. Each stage of the process is preceded by a long-drawn-out emotional crescendo. In the first stage the game 'Bringing up Baby' involves the recital of sentimental details concerning the imaginary son's birth and childhood. George encourages this process until it reaches a peak, when he begins to intone the Requiem Mass:

MARTHA: ... beautiful, beautiful boy.
GEORGE: Absolve, Domine, animas omnium fidelium ...
(Act III, p.129)

This is the first stage; the mood then changes. The violent recriminations which follow reach a similar peak, and again George begins to intone the words of the Requiem Mass. Though Honey knows what George means, Martha has not gathered the significance of this gesture. There follows the announcement itself which is spun out for an agonisingly long time (Act III, pp.134−5). Suspending the actual announcement in this way greatly increases its effect. Thus the final act is constructed to eclipse the false climax of Act II and thus to constitute the 'exorcism' of their former manner of life. Without this skilful control of structure in the manipulation and graduation of successive climaxes, such an effect could hardly have been achieved.

Style

Physical action in the play is confined to the pretended murder with a fake gun, the smashed bottle, the dancing scene and the scuffle. Off stage there is the unsuccessful sexual encounter between Nick and Martha. There is, therefore, an unusual dependence upon talk. The concentration upon quarrelling and repartee in this play demands that it should not only be vital, but also diversified. In this respect Albee is notably successful. The play has a consistently brilliant verbal surface, full of energy and variety. When the play was first produced, the quality in the dialogue that attracted most attention was its obscenity. Albee makes free with language which in 1962 was not generally acceptable on the public stage. The use of such language gave the play a shock value it can now no longer have. But in 1962 the abandon and ferocity of the chief characters was powerfully conveyed by this means.

Another quality which enlivens the dialogue is its sheer brilliance and swiftness of repartee. Martha and George are well-practised opponents, and both are highly educated. As a result, in spite of its frequent obscenity, their quarrelling is not merely vulgar. George, as the most educated character, is pre-eminent in this respect, but Martha is not far behind. Examples are not far to seek. The account of

Martha's courtship of George is characteristic of her destructive energy (Act I, p.54). As an example of the mixture of coarseness and wit we might cite Martha's taunting of Nick after their unsuccessful encounter (Act III, p.111). This dismisses his excuse that he's been drinking. The contrast she makes between 'potential' and 'performance' in this context unmistakably gives the stamp of an educated speaker, as does the change in meaning she gives to the word 'potential'. Such examples could be multiplied endlessly.

Brilliant repartee, however, becomes fatiguing in excess. Albee diversifies his dialogue by devices designed to vary the pace and change the tone. One such device is the long uninterrupted narrative, which is particularly effective. For example, a long conversation between George and Nick is divided by a long narrative (Act II, p.61). This recollection from George's youth has no connection with the preceding conversation, yet is it strangely portentous and arresting, demanding a response. But exactly what response it demands is not clear. The violent elements, such as the shooting of the mother and the driving accident that killed the father, are both told in an oddly parenthetic way as mere asides. The point in the first part of the story seems to be merely sentimental reminiscence, that it was the grandest day of his youth. In the second, there is the silence of the boy who has killed his parents. George puts the emphasis on this silence: 'I'm told that for these thirty years he has ... not ... uttered ... one ... sound.' Not only the length but the apparent inconsequence of the narrative, which seems pointless in the context of the play, serves as a major break in the conversation, allowing it to be prolonged with less danger of tedium.

Set speeches, often ironically rhetorical, are used with the same effect. George, as a lecturer, is the source of most of these; in addition he is a man whose speech is inclined, in Martha's words, to be 'frigging convoluted'. The sardonic mockery of his own style and views implied by his usage is quite in character as well. Examples of these can be found when he speaks of his uncertainties about everything except his son (Act I, p.49) and when he talks about the slow process of civilisation to Nick (Act I, pp.73−4). In both cases these are recognised by the other characters as set speeches, and are ironically applauded as such. They also serve to emphasise the intellectual background of the play: that of uncertainty and a sense of the need to seek a firm basis for living in an era when old landmarks are disappearing.

The last feature of the style which diversifies the dialogue and also contributes indirectly to the main theme has no obvious name, but it is a style of dialogue which Albee shared with writers of the so-called Theatre of the Absurd. This is not to say that either Albee's work in general or this play in particular belongs to this school, which in any case was never closely defined, but he has employed many of the mannerisms of the style, especially in *The American Dream* and *The Sandbox*. In *Who's Afraid of Virginia Woolf?* it only slightly affects the dialogue. It can be seen on those occasions where the dialogue is circular and repetitive to the point of inanity. In any case the drunken state of all the characters and Honey's simplicity of mind demand it. An example occurs when Honey proposes some dancing (Act II, p.78). The word 'dance' is repeated over and over while the actual proposal is advanced but little. Even more striking is the dialogue (Act II, p.96) concerning, first of all, Honey's lying on the bathroom floor. The circumstances of this are repeated and mulled over in a way which suggests not only that she has taken leave of her reason, but that the others have too. Immediately following is Nick's request for ice. The word is repeated six times before George agrees to fetch some, but then does not. The effect of this type of dialogue when used continually is to suggest a world where rational communication is impossible because the world itself has no rational meaning. In this play we are not presented with such a world, but there is a suggestion of radical doubts and uncertainties in an apparently rational world, which such devices serve to underscore.

Closely allied to inane and repetitive dialogue is the use of arresting absurdity, often in connection with a shocking event. The effect of this is to suggest that events, rather than words, have no meaning. Examples can be found on the occasion in George's long narrative (Act II, p.62) when it is a porcupine which causes the car to swerve and crash. Again, when George is talking of their supposed son's death he persuades Honey to confirm that he ate the telegram, adding preposterously, 'like a good boy', which she solemnly repeats (Act III, p.137). But again these are not characteristic of the dialogue as a whole. They serve to introduce a small ingredient of the world of absurdist drama into the world of this play and to diversify the dialogue and lend it extra vitality and interest.

Appraisal

It is not the place of a work such as this to assess the value of this play. The audience must decide whether or not it commands their interest and then consider whether it has enduring worth. Personal taste will determine, for example, the acceptability of such abandon in abuse and obscenity. As Sir John Gielgud said in an interview with Albee,* 'Ugliness is made a fetish, ugliness and frankness and outspokenness in a way we were brought up to consider was in very bad taste.' In the same interview Albee maintained that shock is a necessary function of

* See footnote on p.9 above.

the theatre (see Part 1, p.9), and Sir John conceded something similar: 'I've always thought that it was one of the responsibilities of playwrights to show people how they are, and what their time is like, in the hope that perhaps they'll change it.'

A further defence of the play's outspokenness could be made on the grounds that this is essential to one of the ideas upon which it is based: that a relationship which has gone as seriously wrong as that between Martha and George can be restored by violent confrontation. Truth for such a relationship, the play seems to say, is necessarily painful; and only by the assertion of truth can 'illusion' be banished. The concept of a therapy of conflict is one about which a reader may well feel doubtful. He is entitled to ask whether outrages and indignities to which each has subjected the other can leave anything of value intact. It is true that the play leaves us in doubt as to the couple's future, but if it does not even suggest that some new beginning is made, one may ask whether their conflict had any value or significance in the first place.

A more serious question which a judgement of the play must necessarily consider is the credibility of its central theme. This is not to ask if we can believe in its central theme as something normal, but whether we can suspend our disbelief for the duration of the play in something admittedly out of the ordinary. If we see the play as a story of a couple whose life is based upon sophisticated game-playing which reaches a point where the games go too far, whereupon a final game ends game-playing for good, then there is no problem. But at the centre of their game-playing is the pretence that they have a son. This pretence is made to bear great emotional weight. The secrecy with which it has hitherto been maintained seems vital to both, so that we have to believe that Martha's revelation of it is a serious outrage. The imaginary life of the 'son' is made the subject of some of their bitterest recriminations. Finally, Martha, whose tolerance of outrage is otherwise considerable, reacts to George's announcement of the 'death' with terror and indignation. Enough has been said elsewhere to indicate the skill with which the theme is presented. But is it inherently credible? To say 'no' is to dismiss the play as having no basis in the world we know. The skilful interweaving of this theme with the wider themes of reality and illusion in the lives of the central couple and in American society at large would then go for nought. Its undoubted energy, its brilliant construction and its fine and varied dialogue would ensure the play's continued popularity none the less.

Part 4

Hints for study

Studying a play

Plays are primarily intended for performance on the stage, not for silent reading. A play depends upon much more for its effect than words alone. The stage sets, the lighting effects and the incidental music are all an integral part of the play's impact. The text may or may not give clear indications of what these should be like. Obviously the appearance and the costumes of the actors are crucial, and again the text may or may not give necessary guidance on this point. The movements of the actors and their positioning on stage are something which the text may not reveal or which may be missed in casual reading. For example, the arrangement of the speeches on the page may not make clear when two quite separate conversations are taking place. The action, gestures and facial expressions that accompany words often make their meaning clearer than the words themselves, especially where irony is involved. And, finally, tone of course may radically affect the meaning of words: the same words may mean totally different things when spoken in different ways. All these are matters upon which playwrights give a varying amount of guidance.

It follows that students of a play will understand it far better if they can see a stage performance. Film versions and taped versions are useful substitutes if this is not possible. To take part in an informal staging of parts of the play or in a dramatic reading is useful, especially with experienced guidance. But if none of these is possible the reader should exercise imagination to envisage what a performance would be like.

Fortunately *Who's Afraid of Virginia Woolf?* is often performed, and there is a film version with Richard Burton and Elizabeth Taylor in the main parts. Furthermore, it is a play which can be approached through the text alone more satisfactorily than many. This is because the scene is confined to one living room whose décor and amenities are specified and give little scope for significant invention (though the incorporation of an American flag into the décor of the original production helped to emphasise, as do their names, that George and Martha are representative of America). The appearance of the characters is documented in the text. George is grey and insignificant looking; Martha is blowzy and overweight and, when she changes, her dress is low-cut and seductive; Nick is blond, handsome and well built; Honey mousy and slim-hipped. Furthermore Albee's stage directions are unusually thorough. They give detailed instructions about facial expression, tone of voice, gesture, movement and action. A characteristic of Albee's stage directions is that they include not only the outward action but the state of mind or motive behind it. Nick's smiles are *'non-committal, tight-lipped'* or even described as *'that small smile again.'* Martha's laughter is characterised according to whether or not her amusement is genuine. Honey's whine is described as *'well-practised'*. In the seduction scene, not only are the outward actions specified in great detail but also the moment at which the feelings of the participants change, and it ceases to be a joke. All these greatly assist a student in an attempt to catch the exact tone and nuance of each speech and action in his or her imagination as the text is read.

Study of the plot and structure

To know a play well involves remembering not only its happenings and dialogues in detail but also its broad outlines and totality. It is possible to have a detailed knowledge without this sense of the overall structure, but a strong sense of the latter is a great help in considering the meaning of the play. It is a useful exercise for a student to tabulate or list the main events of the plot. The summaries in Part 2 of these Notes may be a help but they are much longer and fuller than you need attempt at this stage. The section on 'Structure' in Part 3 may also be read in conjunction with this exercise. There it is pointed out that the titles of the three Acts show the shape and meaning of the plot, and that the four games impose a pattern on it. It would be a good exercise to set out the titles of the three Acts with plenty of space in between, and under these headings to list the following in order, with page references:

(*a*) The four games

(*b*) The stories of
> The boxing match between George and Martha
> Martha's previous marriage
> Her courtship of George
> George's career in the university
> Nick's marriage to Honey
> George's unpublished novel

(*c*) Debates and discussions concerning:
> Nick's sporting and academic achievements
> Biology and its aims
> The return of the 'son'
> Nick's ambitions and strategies
> Nick's 'houseboy' status

(*d*) Physical action:

> George's pretended shooting of Martha
> The broken bottle
> Honey's dance
> Nick and Martha's dance
> The scuffle

Another useful exercise is to prepare a similar page, with the three Acts spaced out vertically down the margin. Across the top of the page insert the four column headings shown below. Then fill in, at the appropriate point in relation to the three Acts, each development in the four major themes:

HEADINGS:

George and Martha	the main confrontations; deadlock; new beginning
Nick and George	the main stages in their conflict
Nick and Martha	the main stages in their flirtation
The 'son'	first mentions; debates concerning him; his 'death'

Fill in with a brief note and page reference to identify each event. Thus, for example, in the 'Nick and Martha' column, you would insert 'Martha changes dress (p.35)' and 'Martha discusses Nick's boxing (pp.38−9)' against Act I.

Two such pages of notes are invaluable for reference in revision.

Study of characters

The characters have all been discussed at length in Part 3 of these Notes. But when you are examining them yourself it can be helpful to divide consideration of a character into the following main headings:

(*a*) *Background*: Basic information concerning their age, circumstances and whatever is known of their history before the play has begun.

(*b*) *Introductory impression*: Dramatists very often prepare for the moment when a character appears on stage by giving advance notice of one quality. Often, too, the character's initial remarks and behaviour confirm this quality. For example, Honey's sexlessness and insipidity, as described by Martha before she arrives, are confirmed by her ineffectual comments and her childish giggle when she appears. These first impressions form a kind of keynote.

(*c*) *Their main qualities*: These are to be sought in the way they behave towards the various characters. Further commentary upon them may be found in what the other characters say about them and what they say about themselves, though naturally either of these, though relevant, may be unreliable. In this play the stage directions reveal much in the way of the character's hidden feelings and motives.

(d) *Their role in relation to the action as a whole*: In this play the characters are so few that none can be seen as even relatively unimportant. Honey is the nearest to a minor character, but the play is inconceivable without her. However, a general rule that the study of a character should not be pursued in isolation, but in relation to the main thrust of the drama, is worth stating even in the case of this play. How, for example, does Honey affect the main theme which concerns George and Martha?

It is helpful, in the study of characters, to mark the text with the initial of the character concerned at each point where something significant for the understanding of that character occurs. Such markings can also be the basis for the memorisation of quotations, which is essential for examinations.

Writing an examination answer

The following instructions are extremely obvious and elementary, but it is surprising how often they are ignored.

1. Answer the question

Everything you say should be contributing in some way to a conclusion which gives an answer to the question. This means that you should avoid the following common mistakes:

(a) *Answering a question which has not been asked*. It may happen that a student is well prepared for a question that is not asked. The prepared material seems too good to waste and so is incorporated into the answer regardless. This is a great mistake. If you are well prepared for a topic that does not come up, think hard and see if any of your material could be relevant to the question set by the examinations. If so, use it. If not, don't. For example, suppose that you are well prepared for an answer on the subject of 'game-playing and illusion' in the play. You are asked to write about 'the play as a critique of American society'. Your material could be used by discussing game-playing and illusion as an indication of decadence. You could point out that although the characters are privileged members of society they are discontented and seek their satisfaction in unnatural ways.

(b) *Simply telling the story of the play*. References to the plot, and individual events within it, should be connected with a line of argument that progresses towards a conclusion which answers the question asked. Events may be referred to by name, rather than recounted in great detail. If, for example, you want to refer to the long story that George tells Nick in Act II, p.61, you could call it 'George's reminiscence of a youthful drinking spree', rather than recounting all its details. Sometimes your answer will necessarily involve a piece of narrative. But as you write it, ask yourself whether all of it is relevant to your line of argument. Cut down to a mimimum those parts that are not, or exclude them.

2. Your answer should be well organised

If an answer is carefully planned it will avoid repetition. Sometimes students repeat the same ideas in different words because they have no more ideas and their essay seems too short. Examiners are not impressed by this. A well-planned answer will lead clearly to a conclusion. The examiner will follow the line of thought, and will see how the student has arrived at his or her conclusion.

Before starting to write, therefore, it is wise to make the following preparations:

(a) Jot down notes of the main points that immediately occur to you. This will, first of all, show you whether you have material enough for an answer.

(b) Work out the paragraph headings into which these points fit. Space these headings out on rough paper and consider what other points come under the same headings.

(c) Think out in what order these points most conveniently may come in your paragraphs.

(d) Think out in what order your paragraphs may come.

(e) Do not include material irrelevant to your paragraph heading.

3. Your answer should be fully illustrated and substantiated from the text

Quotations you have memorised are useful here. Events or particular conversations may be referred to as evidence, either by name or by means of a short summary. Generalisations unsupported by evidence will not impress an examiner.

Some sample questions and answers

1. George claims to hate hypocrisy. How much of his conduct in the play is concerned with exposing it?
2. How would you describe and explain the change that the events of the play make in George and Martha's marriage?

3. The play is primarily concerned with George and Martha's marriage. What contribution do Nick and Honey make to this central theme?
4. How far is the play concerned with criticism of American values?
5. What are the main contrasts between the two married couples, and how significant are they in the play as a whole?
6. Is Honey a minor character, or is her role more significant than it appears to be?
7. 'Truth and illusion, who knows the difference?' Is this what the play is about?
8. George says that there are very few things in the world he is sure of. How much does this theme of uncertainty matter in the play?
9. Is the play fundamentally optimistic or pessimistic?
10. Write an essay on any aspects of Albee's dramatic techniques that have impressed you.

The following are sample answers to four of the above questions. The answers to questions (2) and (8) are given in full, those to questions (3) and (4) in note-form.

2. How would you describe and explain the change that the events of play make in George and Martha's marriage?

At the start of the play it is clear that George and Martha's marriage is beset with difficulties. In the course of the first act we learn what these are. Temperamentally they are opposites: she is outgoing and exuberant, he withdrawn and contemplative. It is typical of her to have prolonged the evening by inviting guests home from her father's party, and typical of him to complain about it. Later in the play we learn that she resents the fact that his lack of dynamism has lost him the chance of succeeding her father as president, the role for which he had been marked out. He in turn resents the domination of his life by her father, and indeed by her. This can be seen when she gives her father's wish as the reason for inviting Nick and Honey back after the party, as though it silenced all possible argument. This is clearly typical. George continually hears of his father-in-law's excellence and his own shortcomings. It is not surprising that he complains to Nick of the emasculating effect of his own position: it involves, he says, the sacrifice 'of a somewhat more private portion of the anatomy'. This weakness on his part drives her to drink and promiscuity. Though this has not broken up their marriage it fills him with disgust and contempt. It also gives him ammunition for counter-attack. 'There aren't many more sickening sights than you with a couple of drinks in you and your skirts up over your head.' Later in the play she concedes his point. 'I disgust me,' she says: 'I pass my life in crummy, totally pointless infidelities,' echoing, later in this speech, his own comment about the skirt over her head. In addition to all this, they are childless.

Although such an account presents an unpromising picture of their marriage, there are certain factors that keep it together. Even in the midst of their violent quarrels it is evident that love is not dead. But the form it takes is unnatural. They have reached a point where quarrels actually nourish their relationship. There is evidence of this in the pleasure they have in each other in the most bitter-sounding exchanges, when she calls him a simpleton and says he has no guts, for example, and when he says she is going bald. George explains their behaviour to Nick, who is bewildered by it, as 'exercising . . . what's left of our wits'. For them it is a kind of game, and such games dominate their lives. Martha admits that what keeps them together is George's expertise in these games. 'George', she says, ' . . . whom I will bite so there's blood; who keeps learning the games we play as quickly as I can change the rules . . .' One of their games is to pretend they have a son. Partly this is compensation for the fact that they have not, and partly it widens the scope of their recriminations. For example, in the course of the play Martha taunts George with uncertainty about the child's father: George accuses Martha of having driven the boy from home by her sexual advances.

The arrival of guests introduces a new element. Played out publicly, their games have a new dimension and a new danger. Nick is a threat to George: his professional drive and his masculinity both attract Martha who openly taunts George with the comparison they invite. Her account of George's humiliation, such as the 'boxing match' and the unpublished novel, combine with a flirtation that is undisguised and increasingly serious. George successfully retaliates by exposing Nick in the game of 'Get the Guests'. This effectively destroys Martha's success in winning him. At this point they admit they have reached the point of no return and declare 'total war'. But the decisive element in bringing their warfare to this point is the matter of the imaginary son. By speaking to Honey about their 'son', Martha has defied George's warning and broken their tacit agreement that their fantasy should not be publicised. The seriousness of this act is indicated by George's reaction when he learns of it: Albee's stage directions specify that he reacts with extreme shock.

The emotional depth of this pretence is also made clear by the violence of the mutual recriminations that centre on the 'son', and finally the shock and fury with which she receives the news of his 'death'. George deliberately works up Martha's thwarted maternal emotions before making the announcement so that the purgation it effects is as complete as possible.

What precisely is the change that Albee means us to think this has effected? Obviously this particular pretence is at an end, just as the destructive games they have played are brought to an end with Act II when they become all too real. The closing scene of the play shows both characters feeling exposed and nervous at the prospect of life without illusion. There is no suggestion that the original problems of their marriage such as their childlessness, George's failure, the dominating father-in-law and Martha's heavy drinking will disappear. The realities from which they no longer will escape are not reassuring. But there is a new found complicity in facing them together. They emphasise that their childlessness was a joint failure when Nick asks them: the stage directions specify '*a hint of communion*' in the way they do so. Moreover, Martha, who had complained that she 'wore the pants' because no one else would, has now acknowledged George's leadership. She had pleaded with him before to distinguish between truth and illusion. Now he has done so. It is he, too, who sounds the optimistic note, assuring her that things will be better. Finally the choice of truth as against illusion is an act of faith. They have acted on the assumption that truth and integrity matter. This gives them a basis, however ill-defined, that their lives had previously lacked.

---

8. George says that there are very few things in the world he is sure of. How much does this theme of uncertainty matter in the play?

In the speech where George says that he is sure of very little in the world, the one thing about which he does express certainty is untrue, namely that he is the father of a son. Uncertainty is part of the mood of this play: it was the climate of opinion in which Albee was writing, and it is the backcloth against which the personal drama of the two couples is played out. It is present as a theme in the foreground as well. We may divide the uncertainties of the play into three areas: political and social, religious and metaphysical, and finally personal and psychological.

Political and social uncertainty characterised the period immediately before Albee wrote the play. It was the time of the Cold War. There is a reference to this when George rather wildly invites Nick (whose name, Albee tells us, was chosen to link him with the Russian leader Nikita Khrushchev) to join him in an alliance against the Chinese, meaning that America and Russia would defeat China and divide the spoils. George, an historian, has an obsession with totalitarian utopias whether they are real, like Communist Russia, or imagined, like the biological utopia for which he accuses Nick of working. For him they are a threat to the civilisation he knows and values. He makes two ironic speeches on the subject: one to the assembled company where he praises its variety and unpredictability (symbolised for him by decadent Berlin), and to Nick when he speaks of its slow growth and the connections between morality and government. However, although he is aware of totalitarianism as a threat to his society he is not optimistic or uncritical about it. He laughs *'ruefully'* as he reads from Spengler's *Decline of the West*, sharing its pessimism. He is a New Englander who regards the mid-Western Nick as uncouth, mimicking his accent ('champeen') and mocking his life story as 'bucolic'. Yet, if the mid-West seems uncouth to him, his native New England appears decadent. New Englanders carefully saved their skins during the Second World War when civilisation was at stake. He agrees that New Englanders, and all other Americans, drink heavily. And in his immediate environment, the university, this decadence is no less in evidence: he derides the 'orgies' of the faculty and compares the faculty wives to South American prostitutes. The importance of this theme should not be exaggerated: only George, the historian, speaks of it, but it is present and Albee had a purpose in referring to it.

The second area of uncertainty, the religious and metaphysical, affects both background and foreground. Religion is not a major theme of the play, but there are substantial references to it which cannot be accidental. There may be significance in the use of our Lord's name as a swear-word at the beginning and end of the first Act. It is certainly not out of place in the godless environment to which we are introduced. More significant is Martha's comment that she was an atheist at her convent school, and the uncertainty with which she says she still is. The religion represented by Honey's father is clearly not to be taken seriously: it is corrupted by showmanship, profiteering and sex. The Roman Catholic church, however, which educated Martha, is not so dismissed. It is with the rites of the Roman Church that the 'son' is symbolically buried, though there is no suggestion that George is a believer; indeed a believer might consider his use of the rite blasphemous in context. But it does undoubtedly express for him the momentousness of what he is doing. The main characters then are not presented either as believers or unbelievers. This mood, or climate of opinion, in which the question is raised but not answered is characteristic of Greenwich Village in Albee's apprentice years, and in that climate of opinion this uncertainty included philosophy as well as religion. Truth and illusion are a central theme in the play. The words are frequently repeated in various forms: as a challenge, for example, when George tells a story which Nick questions; as a reproach when Martha says George doesn't know the difference or doesn't care; or in generalisations as when George says that even if we cannot tell the difference, we should act as if we could, and that all truth is relative anyway. Our attention is further drawn to this theme by the introduction of several stories whose truthfulness is left in doubt.

George's story of the boy who accidentally killed both parents is an example; the exact history of Honey's pregnancy or pregnancies is another. But the main importance of this theme is in the action of the play itself. Illusion is exposed and truth established in the lives of both main and secondary characters. George and Martha finally choose a life without 'illusion' when George 'kills' their son. This theme is duplicated in the lives of Nick and Honey in that the truths about them are exposed and their respectable façade shattered.

It is, of course, on personal and psychological questions that the play concentrates. Where the political, social and metaphysical bases of life are uncertain, individuals are forced to make their own certainties. It is part of the existentialism with which Albee was familiar that individuals make their own meaning in an otherwise meaningless universe. But if the universe is meaningless any such 'meaning' is an illusion. On the personal and psychological level, both pairs of characters cling to illusions about themselves and George and Martha use game-playing also, to evade reality. The truths of Nick and Honey's marriage are concealed behind the pretence that he is a chivalrous and protective husband, she a demure and respectable little wife. George ruthlessly exposes them. George blames his failures on the emasculating effect of his position: Martha excuses her lack of self-control in the belief that she is good-hearted 'beneath the barnacles'. They each expose the other, brutally and articulately, at the end of Act II. Again, they take refuge from the sordid realities of their marriage by turning real conflict into a sado-masochistic game. This game gets out of hand, and by involving others, becomes real and brings them to an impasse. And lastly they escape the reality of their childlessness by the fantasy of a 'son'.

If the theme of uncertainty had not this personal and psychological dimension, we might conclude that it was part of the intellectual a mosphere of the time, and therefore, inevitably, reflected in the c onversation of the characters. It would be incidental only. But it is not only in the background. It affects the lives of both couples. The uncertainties of life make illusion an attractive escape route. By the end of the play, that way of escape is barred, at least for Martha and George.

---

3. The play is primarily concerned with George and Martha's marriage. What contribution do Nick and Honey make to this central theme?

Paragraph 1 Comparison of status of the two couples in the play

    (*a*) Play begins and ends with George and Martha alone

    (*b*) Honey absent from stage for much of the play

    (*c*) Little conversation between Nick and Honey

Paragraph 2   What happens to the marriage of the central couple (see sample answer to question 2)

(*a*) Their discontents and the causes
(*b*) Their games/conflicts
(*c*) Their fantasy of a son
(*d*) Their deadlock, and the 'death' of the 'son'
(*e*) The effect of (*d*) for their future

Paragraph 3   How Nick and Honey are essential to this process

(*a*) Their presence causes conflict to escalate, e.g.:
　　(i) Martha's stories about George
　　(ii) Martha's flirtation with Nick
(*b*) Their role as audience:
　　(i) To the story of the 'son'
　　(ii) To George's announcement of his 'death'

Paragraph 4   How Nick and Honey are affected by this process

(*a*) Nick is exposed (See the section on his character in Part 3.)
(*b*) Honey is changed – desire for children (How significant is this?)
(*c*) The truths about them are revealed. He unchanged, she changed

Paragraph 5   Conclusions. Nick and Honey are essential to the central theme because:

(*a*) They are catalysts of the changes in George and Martha (refer to your paragraphs 2 and 3)
(*b*) They duplicate the main theme in their own lives:
　　(i) The truth about them is revealed, the illusion destroyed
　　(ii) Honey is a changed person

---

4. How far is the play concerned with criticism of American values?

Paragraph 1   Albee's interest in social criticism

What have you learnt from these Notes about Albee's attitude to American society? (See Part 1)

Paragraph 2   Social background of the play

(*a*) Barbarism of mid-West. (See the sections on 'Background and setting' and on Nick's character in Part 3 of these Notes.) What qualities does Albee seem to hold up for our criticism? Where are they in evidence?
(*b*) Decadence of New England. (See the section on 'Background and setting' and on George's character in Part 3.) What signs are there of this?

Paragraph 3   Qualities singled out for criticism

(*a*) Consumerism. (See the sections on Martha's character and on 'Materialism and success worship' in Part 3.)

(*b*) Ambition and power lust. (See the sections on Nick's character and on 'Materialism and success worship' in Part 3.)

(*c*) Sterility. In both couples (voluntary and involuntary). Are these seen as typical American faults or peculiar to these characters?

Paragraph 4   How central these are to the main direction of the plot

(*a*) They contribute to the discontent of George and Martha's marriage.

(*b*) Ambition and power lust are the subject of Nick's exposure. Sterility is the source of the main 'illusion' that is exposed, and the area in which Honey is changed.

Paragraph 5   Is the theme of truth and illusion a moral for America or not? Consider:

(*a*) The 'representative' nature of the play; for example the names, the décor in the original production

(*b*) The fact that no society is free of self-delusion

(*c*) That our main concentration could be on the characters as individuals, without excluding the possibility of wider social reference

Part 5

Suggestions for further reading

The text

The edition of Edward Albee's *Who's Afraid of Virginia Woolf?* used in these Notes is that published by Penguin Books, Harmondsworth, in 1965 and subsequently reprinted sixteen times. A paperback edition of the text is published in the U.S.A. by Atheneum, New York, 1962.

Other works by the author

Zoo Story, Coward, McCann & Geoghegan, New York, 1960; Samuel French, London, 1963.

The Death of Bessie Smith, Coward, McCann & Geoghegan, New York 1960; Samuel French, London, 1962.

The Sandbox, Coward, McCann & Geoghegan, New York, 1960; with *Zoo Story*, *The Death of Bessie Smith*, Jonathan Cape, London, 1962.

The American Dream, Coward, McCann & Geoghegan, 1961; Samuel French, London, 1962.

Tiny Alice, Atheneum, New York, 1965; Jonathan Cape, London, 1966.

A Delicate Balance, Atheneum, New York 1966; Penguin Books, Harmondsworth, 1969.

Quotations from Mao Tse Tung, with *The Box*, Atheneum, New York, 1968.

All Over, Atheneum, New York, 1971.

The Lady from Dubuque, Atheneum, New York, 1980.

The first four works listed above will be of particular use to the student looking at Albee's development up to the production of *Who's Afraid of Virginia Woolf?*

Theatrical background

In order to see Albee's work in context the following are recommended. Both comment usefully on Albee's work.

ESSLIN, MARTIN: *The Theatre of the Absurd*, Eyre & Spottiswoode, London, 1962.
NICOLL, ALLARDYCE: *World Drama*, Harrap, London, 1962.

Criticism

BIGSBY, C.W.E.: *Albee*, 'Writers and Critics' series, Oliver & Boyd, Edinburgh and London, 1969. This has a good section on Albee's life and juvenilia.
BIGSBY, C.W.E. (ED.): *Edward Albee: A Collection of Critical Essays*, 'Twentieth Century Views' series, Prentice-Hall, Englewood Cliffs, N.J., 1975. This contains some of the best criticism on Albee in general and on particular plays, including *Who's Afraid of Virginia Woolf?*
HAYMAN, R: *Edward Albee*, Heinemann Educational, London, 1972. A useful introductory book, discussing plays individually.
WAGER, W. (ED.): *The Playwrights Speak*, Longman, London, 1967. This contains Albee's own views in recorded interviews.

The author of these notes

CHRISTOPHER HUDSON was educated at Brasenose College, Oxford where he read English Language and Literature and graduated in 1961. After two years in Nigeria he returned to Oxford and read for the degree of B.Phil. Since then he has lectured in Universities in Ethiopia, Madagascar, Saudi Arabia and Egypt. He was also, briefly, a master at Bedford School.

York Notes: list of titles

CHINUA ACHEBE
Things Fall Apart
EDWARD ALBEE
Who's Afraid of Virginia Woolf?
ANONYMOUS
Beowulf
Everyman
W. H. AUDEN
Selected Poems
JANE AUSTEN
Emma
Mansfield Park
Northanger Abbey
Persuasion
Pride and Prejudice
Sense and Sensibility
SAMUEL BECKETT
Waiting for Godot
ARNOLD BENNETT
The Card
JOHN BETJEMAN
Selected Poems
WILLIAM BLAKE
Songs of Innocence, Songs of Experience
ROBERT BOLT
A Man For All Seasons
HAROLD BRIGHOUSE
Hobson's Choice
ANNE BRONTË
The Tenant of Wildfell Hall
CHARLOTTE BRONTË
Jane Eyre
EMILY BRONTË
Wuthering Heights
ROBERT BROWNING
Men and Women
JOHN BUCHAN
The Thirty-Nine Steps
JOHN BUNYAN
The Pilgrim's Progress
BYRON
Selected Poems
GEOFFREY CHAUCER
Prologue to the Canterbury Tales
The Clerk's Tale
The Franklin's Tale
The Knight's Tale
The Merchant's Tale
The Miller's Tale
The Nun's Priest's Tale

The Pardoner's Tale
The Wife of Bath's Tale
Troilus and Criseyde
SAMUEL TAYLOR COLERIDGE
Selected Poems
SIR ARTHUR CONAN DOYLE
The Hound of the Baskervilles
WILLIAM CONGREVE
The Way of the World
JOSEPH CONRAD
Heart of Darkness
STEPHEN CRANE
The Red Badge of Courage
BRUCE DAWE
Selected Poems
DANIEL DEFOE
Moll Flanders
Robinson Crusoe
WALTER DE LA MARE
Selected Poems
SHELAGH DELANEY
A Taste of Honey
CHARLES DICKENS
A Tale of Two Cities
Bleak House
David Copperfield
Great Expectations
Hard Times
Oliver Twist
The Pickwick Papers
EMILY DICKINSON
Selected Poems
JOHN DONNE
Selected Poems
GERALD DURRELL
My Family and Other Animals
GEORGE ELIOT
Middlemarch
Silas Marner
The Mill on the Floss
T. S. ELIOT
Four Quartets
Murder in the Cathedral
Selected Poems
The Cocktail Party
The Waste Land
J. G. FARRELL
The Siege of Krishnapur
WILLIAM FAULKNER
The Sound and the Fury

HENRY FIELDING
Joseph Andrews
Tom Jones

F. SCOTT FITZGERALD
Tender is the Night
The Great Gatsby

GUSTAVE FLAUBERT
Madame Bovary

E. M. FORSTER
A Passage to India
Howards End

JOHN FOWLES
The French Lieutenant's Woman

JOHN GALSWORTHY
Strife

MRS GASKELL
North and South

WILLIAM GOLDING
Lord of the Flies
The Spire

OLIVER GOLDSMITH
She Stoops to Conquer
The Vicar of Wakefield

ROBERT GRAVES
Goodbye to All That

GRAHAM GREENE
Brighton Rock
The Heart of the Matter
The Power and the Glory

WILLIS HALL
The Long and the Short and the Tall

THOMAS HARDY
Far from the Madding Crowd
Jude the Obscure
Selected Poems
Tess of the D'Urbervilles
The Mayor of Casterbridge
The Return of the Native
The Woodlanders

L. P. HARTLEY
The Go-Between

NATHANIEL HAWTHORNE
The Scarlet Letter

SEAMUS HEANEY
Selected Poems

ERNEST HEMINGWAY
A Farewell to Arms
The Old Man and the Sea

SUSAN HILL
I'm the King of the Castle

BARRY HINES
Kes

HOMER
The Iliad
The Odyssey

GERARD MANLEY HOPKINS
Selected Poems

TED HUGHES
Selected Poems

ALDOUS HUXLEY
Brave New World

HENRIK IBSEN
A Doll's House

HENRY JAMES
The Portrait of a Lady
Washington Square

BEN JONSON
The Alchemist
Volpone

JAMES JOYCE
A Portrait of the Artist as a Young Man
Dubliners

JOHN KEATS
Selected Poems

PHILIP LARKIN
Selected Poems

D. H. LAWRENCE
Selected Short Stories
Sons and Lovers
The Rainbow
Women in Love

HARPER LEE
To Kill a Mocking-Bird

LAURIE LEE
Cider with Rosie

CHRISTOPHER MARLOWE
Doctor Faustus

HERMAN MELVILLE
Moby Dick

THOMAS MIDDLETON and
WILLIAM ROWLEY
The Changeling

ARTHUR MILLER
A View from the Bridge
Death of a Salesman
The Crucible

JOHN MILTON
Paradise Lost I & II
Paradise Lost IV & IX
Selected Poems

V. S. NAIPAUL
A House for Mr Biswas

ROBERT O'BRIEN
Z for Zachariah

SEAN O'CASEY
Juno and the Paycock

GEORGE ORWELL
Animal Farm
Nineteen Eighty-four